Praise for

Mom & M~·

My Journey with Mom's S.

"This is a story of a girl growing up with a mother who gradually develops a serious mental illness, schizophrenia, and who becomes impossible to live with. First impossible, and then a heavy emotional burden. In the end, it is a story of hope. Alexandra Georgas is witness to the possibilities that human beings have of healing the persons they love."

—Mary V. Seeman, OC MDCM
Professor Emerita Dept. of Psychiatry
University of Toronto

"Living with mental illness shapes everyone in the family, often in unexpected ways. Alexandra Georgas tells the story of her and her mother's shared journey with schizophrenia. It is a story of despair and hope, of letting go and holding on. Most of all, it is a tale of hard-won resilience."

—Meg Wallace,
freelance book editor,
graduate student in social work at Baylor University

"At Thresholds we know how invaluable a family member support system can be in creating recovery for persons experiencing mental illnesses. It's difficult to share the story of how mental illness has touched your family, so I applaud each person like Alexandra who bravely does so."

—Mark Ishaug,
CEO, Thresholds

"It is a mark against us as a society that schizophrenia remains such a stigmatised malady. Many countries around the world have closed down large mental hospitals and people with schizophrenia are now largely living in the community. Yet many remain with a feeling of lack of engagement with society and much of that feeling mirrors stigmatised views about schizophrenia. Sadly, it is also the case that family members, whilst having to deal with what can be a difficult journey and illness in their loved one, also feel that lack of societal inclusion. Thus, anyone brave enough to tell their story as a family member of someone with schizophrenia, is to be commended. I hope this book, a true life story, will be a rich and rewarding read and will help people understand the person apart from the illness and also appreciate the way it touches family members."

—Dr. David J. Castle,
Chair of Psychiatry, St. Vincent's Hospital,
The University of Melbourne, Victoria, Australia

"*Mom and Me* is a treasure of a book for so many reasons. In chronicling life with her mentally ill mother, Alexandra Georgas provides a vivid portrait, rich in everyday details, of the devastating impact of schizophrenia on families and society. The author also illustrates the role of a vibrant faith in dealing with personal tragedy. Further, she provides hope for individuals and families who struggle with serious mental illness. I read this captivating story in one sitting. I highly recommend this gem of a book to anyone affected by serious mental illness, which is pretty much all of us."

—Robert J. Gregory
Professor Emeritus of Psychology
Wheaton College, Illinois

"With care, candor, and humor, Alexandra tells the extraordinary story of growing up with her mom, a beautiful woman who struggles with the illness of schizophrenia. Alexandra interweaves poems, songs, and diary entries from her younger years with insights gained as an adult to create a deeply meaningful story. Her book has the power to foster empathy among those unfamiliar with schizophrenia and strength in those who have a loved one with mental illness. It raises awareness not only of the needs of the mentally ill, and our shared social responsibility to care for them well, but also of the needs of their families. Superbly intelligent, Alexandra writes in a simple style that most readers will understand easily, in tones rich with generosity, humility, faith, and forgiveness, but most of all, with a clear emphasis on the transformative power of love to bring healing. Her life-story is a gift."

—Jane Beal, PhD
> Associate Researcher in English
> University of California, Davis
> sanctuarypoet.net

"The author has embraced the healing power of personal narrative to frame and integrate her experiences living with a mother with schizophrenia. She describes the good times and the bad, underscores the importance of advocacy, and provides evidence of the positive impact of spirituality in her life. Through her journey, she learned a great deal about her mother and even more about herself."

—Joanne Nicholson, Ph.D.
> Professor of Psychiatry
> The Geisel School of Medicine at Dartmouth
> Lebanon, New Hampshire

"Oftentimes individuals with a serious mental illness such as schizophrenia alienate family members leading them to living a lonely life with minimal to no family involvement. This is a story of the unconditional love a daughter has for her mother who is dealing with the debilitating symptoms of schizophrenia. Alexandra Georgas shares her inspiring journey on the road to acceptance and a happy relationship with her mom".

> **—Catherine Cox,** MSW, LCSW
> Master of Social Work (MSW)
> Licensed Clinical Social Worker (LCSW)

"A story of love and its redemptive power to transform loss, pain, and bewilderment into peace, wisdom, and belonging."

> **—Ruth Goring,**
> poet, author of *Soap Is Political*

"Wow—when Alexandra says: "My Journey with Mom's Schizophrenia", she really means it! She has re-captured the overwhelming impact of what it is like to live with one's primary caretaker who has a severe, debilitating mental illness!

For anyone who wants to know what it is like—this book is 'must reading'. For anyone who as gone through a similar journey themselves—and is shattered from the chaos—this book is 'must reading'. For any mental health professional that wants to know what the impact of mental illness is on family members—this book is a 'must reading'.

We often struggle to emotionally thrive when people we love are incapable of emotionally thriving themselves. We often feel that *we* are not allowed to emotionally thrive if they can't. This book will surely help others with their struggle to have a healthy relationship with a loved one who is incapable of having a healthy realtionship!"

—Steve Eisenberg, MS, LCPC,

Counseling & Psychotherapy Private Practice
Adj. Faculty, Masters in Clin. Psych. Program,
Benedictine University

Mom & Me:
My Journey with Mom's Schizophrenia
by Alexandra Georgas

© Copyright 2016 Alexandra Georgas

ISBN 978-1-63393-279-1

All rights reserved. No part of this publication may be reproduced, stored in a retrieval system, or transmitted in any form or by any means – electronic, mechanical, photocopy, recording, or any other – except for brief quotations in printed reviews, without the prior written permission of the author.

Published by

 köehlerbooks™

210 60th Street
Virginia Beach, VA 23451
800-435-4811
www.koehlerbooks.com

Prescott Valley Public Library

Mom & Me

My Journey with Mom's Schizophrenia

ALEXANDRA GEORGAS

VIRGINIA BEACH
CAPE CHARLES

Table of Contents

Chapter 1

THE CALL

*"Schizophrenia is considered the most
severe psychiatric disorder."*[1]

THE CALL CAME in the middle of the night, around 2 a.m.

"Hello," I answered. I was only nineteen.

"Yeah, hi." The cop spoke in a calloused Chicago accent. "This is the Carol Stream Police. Is this Sandy Georgas?"

"Yes," I admitted with trepidation and a creeping sense of dread.

"Is your mother Susan Georgas?"

"Yes." Visions of various tragedies flooded my imagination as I braced for the officer's news.

"Yeah, your mother tried to kill herself tonight. She jumped off her fourth-floor balcony and is now in Central DuPage Hospital. She's pretty banged up but she's alive. She'd like to see you."

I gasped, hardly able to breathe, let alone speak. I was shocked. A cloud of anxiety was quickly forming in my stomach. Trying to disbelieve but failing, I swirled in a mixture of teenage

---

1   Abraham Rudnick and David Row, "Diagnostic Interviewing," in *Clinical Handbook of Schizophrenia*, ed. Kim T. Mueser and Dilip V. Jeste (New York: Guilford, 2008), 117; William B. Lawson, "Schizophrenia in African Americans," in *Clinical Handbook of Schizophrenia,* ed. Kim T. Mueser and Dilip V. Jeste (New York: Guilford, 2008), 616.

embarrassment and anger—mostly anger—that the officer had delivered his devastating message in such an unpeaceful and uncaring way.

After I thanked the officer and hung up, I sat motionless, stuck in space. I wanted to be numb, but I wasn't. Fear and sadness were building in my gut. But before I let a torrent of tears loose, I knew I had to do what I always did in my many life crises. I called Mary.

My lifelong best friend was just one year younger than me. How could I have survived my childhood without her? She was always my refuge, my comforter, my haven of rest. She was God in child form, giving me love like no one else.

Mary came immediately. She walked through our connecting back yards, entered my home, and wrapped her skinny, loving arms tightly around me. Now I was free to cry. Mary caught every tear with her tender love until I could speak, then she listened intently as I reiterated to her the short conversation with the cop. It felt good that I was no longer alone with the news. Thanks to Mary, I was never alone.

"What are you going to do?" Mary asked.

"I need to be there with her." I said. "I need to go see her."

I woke Dad and asked if I could borrow his car so I could drive to the hospital. Of course, he said it was no problem. Beyond that, he seemed at a loss for words. I suppose he was shocked, but because my parents were now divorced, he didn't have to do anything. She wasn't his problem anymore. No, she was mine, all mine. It didn't matter that I was still a kid. I had to be the adult, as well as a teenager could be. Divorce is great for the parents, I thought. They get to walk away from all the conflict. But that just dumps it on the kids, who get to deal with it on their own. At least, that was my situation.

In the hospital emergency room, Mom was lying motionless and naked under a thin blanket on a cold table. She was conscious, but her beautiful brown eyes were glossy, perhaps from the pain medicine they had given her, or from alcohol still in her bloodstream. Her hair, which she always kept so perfectly set, was tousled with leaves and grass intertwined in her curls. Her body was dirty, no doubt from the ground she collided with to end her fall. She said nothing, just stared into my eyes.

I wanted to cry, but instead I pushed down the emotions in order to be strong for her. She needed me. Once again, I had to be the adult, the mother. And because I loved her so immensely, I felt honored to give her my love in that dark hour. My shock had to be dismissed. The fear, the fact I had no idea what was happening or what to do—all of it—had to be postponed.

Somehow I figured out what to say. I grabbed her hand and held it tightly and looked her in the eyes. With tears sneaking into the corners of my own eyes, I whispered, "Mom, I'm so glad you didn't die because I love you. I'm so glad you're still here. I'm just so glad you are here. I love you."

She said nothing, just fixed her gaze on me. She looked lost and seemed to be saying, *Get me through this, Sandy, by giving me a reason to live. Be here with me.* So I was. I felt comforted in my own pain by being there to help her with hers.

When Mom's live-in boyfriend, Bill, showed up at the hospital, he stood on the other side of the cold table and demanded repetitively, "Suzy, why'd you do that? Why'd you do that, Suzy? Suzy, why'd you do that?" The obvious guilt in his tone conveyed that he was trying to convince me he had nothing to do with this. But I knew he had gambled away her last penny and had treated her cruelly. I hated him, and I hated it that he was there. Mom glanced over at him, said nothing, then returned her gaze to me.

Frustrated, Bill left. I was relieved. After about twenty minutes, Mom finally spoke, slowly and fearfully. "Is Bill still there?" She had been looking at me so intently, she hadn't even noticed that he was gone. I felt badly that she had suffered emotionally just thinking that he was there nineteen minutes longer than he was. "No, Mom. He's gone. It's just me. I'm here." I squeezed her hand to emphasize my presence with her. It was one of the most bonding moments I had ever had with my mother. I was so glad to give her comfort, to be there for this woman who had done so much for me but now was in so much trouble.

I was later told that Mom had broken her leg and hip and had fractured four ribs. Her body was never the same after that; nor was her life. For the rest of her days she would walk with a limp and suffer chronic physical pain. But her life was yet to take an even more dramatic change, in some ways for the worse. Still, in many ways the fall saved her.

Chapter 2

BEFORE

"The brain has been estimated to contain
10,000,000,000,000 cells."[2]

MOM WAS BEAUTIFUL. Some people said she looked like Elizabeth Taylor, with her pretty face framed by short, curled brown hair. Mom always kept herself very presentable, always wearing makeup, and just the right blend. Mary's mother used to comment that she looked nice even when she was working in her many flower gardens. Though Mom's weight yo-yoed and she was usually on the plump side, she looked good no matter how much she weighed.

Mom was also a fabulous seamstress. I watched her sew many a 1960s pantsuit on her old Singer machine, and she gave my Barbie an incredible wardrobe that she

My pretty young mom.

---

2   Nancy C. Andreasen, *The Broken Brain*, (New York: Harper Perennial, 1984), 125.

put together on that old contraption. Mom loved to accent her creations with pom-poms and rickrack, which were the rave back then. Too bad she didn't give them up when they went out of style in the 1970s.

As a child, I especially loved it when Mom made me an outfit to match hers. I remember the red polka-dot dress with the round neck, red waistband and lace along the knee-length hem. I felt so pretty in that dress. Then there was the powder-blue polyester pantsuit with the big gold-buckled belt that I proudly wore next to Mom's identical adult-sized version. Back then, I wanted to look and be like Mom.

Mom and I wearing matching polyester suits she made.

Mom's sewing machine used to be in my bedroom, which turned out to be a bad thing for me. The old black Singer didn't work well, and she fought with it as she produced her creations. This was the only time I heard Mom swear—when she was frustrated with the unreliable device. "Son of a bitch" and "bastard" were her two favorite expressions, and I heard them far too often. Looking back, I wonder if she was actually expressing anger at Dad, who was too cheap to buy her a better machine. Mom loved to pretend everything was fine. But things weren't, and not just with that stupid Singer.

The other bad part about having her Singer in my room was when I stepped on those damn pins. I can't count the number of times I yelled in pain as the sharp pins dug deep into the bottom of my foot. But being a human pincushion wasn't anywhere near as painful as the emotional wounds of my childhood. In comparison, a pinprick was just a minor irritant.

Mom had her odd and spacey times. One day the whole family was packed up and ready to go to downtown Chicago to watch the Bears play. We were going with a group from Dad's work and had to be at his workplace on time or we'd miss the bus to the city. As we were driving to the meet-up location, Mom screamed out in the car, "I forgot our lunches at home! We have to go back!" I was thinking, "Can't we just buy food there?" Dad and Mom fought for a while, and somehow we ended up turning around and going home. We didn't see the Bears play, not even on TV. I was perplexed about that day. Don't they sell food at Soldier Field? It was a hint of something amiss in my parents' world—something I didn't understand until much later.

Mom seemed to have achieved a good number of victories over Dad. One day when Mom and I were alone, she confessed to me that Dad wasn't keen about spending their limited funds on piano lessons for me, though I loved taking them. But she had pleaded and negotiated a deal. They owned a three-flat apartment building that yielded three dollars a week in quarters from the small laundry facility in the building, "Dad was against your lessons but I got him to agree," Mom told me with pride. "That laundry money is just enough every week to pay for your lessons!" I got to study for seven years on those weekly washing machine quarters, thanks to Mom.

When Mom and I were going somewhere in the car together, she would confide in me, telling me little stories of the distresses in her life. "I joined a gym," she said one day. "Really, wow. That's great!" I responded. "But your father found out and made me quit." I was stunned and didn't know what to say to that. I stayed quiet. I was imagining the argument that must have taken place behind their bedroom door. I was sure it wasn't a pleasant one. Now as an adult, I can see the many issues this conflict hinted at. Why couldn't she just tell Dad she was going to a gym? Why wouldn't he be happy for her? Why wouldn't he support her in that? Mom seemed unhappy about being unable to do what she wanted to do. There must have been a lot more going on than one argument about a gym membership.

Every year at school we would have our Christmas party, with its infamous grab bag. When I was in sixth grade, Mom did her motherly duty once again, and as I left for school, she handed me the present I was to give that morning. What I didn't know was that under the colorful red paper was a gift appropriate for a girl much younger than twelve. As the recipient opened my gift, a pink plastic hairbrush and play makeup set, she looked sickened and disgusted. "Who gave this?" the girl demanded with disdain. "Ah, I did," I sheepishly admitted. "This is for a *little* girl!" she pronounced. All the other girls stared at me in full condemnation: I had insulted all of them. The pack leader then declared in resigned disappointment, "I'll give it to my little sister." I was utterly humiliated, and I hadn't even picked out the gift.

Back home the door was barely open before I yelled, "Mom! The gift you bought was for a little girl. They all made fun of me for it." And I burst into tears. After a few repeats of the details, Mom began tearing up herself. She felt terrible that she had misjudged my age group and gotten the grab bag gift so wrong. "I'm sorry honey," she said sweetly. Then I felt badly to have made her so upset. I found myself caught between being comforted by her apology and feeling guilty that I had wounded her in the process. My focus turned to tending to her. I just wanted to make her feel better. It was one of the first times we experienced the role reversal that would come to define our relationship permanently within just a few years, in which I was more concerned about her emotions than my own.

Mom had a beautiful singing voice, and she often sang show tunes around the house. My only sibling, Ted, four years older than me, jokes even today about how we knew every line of the soundtracks to *The Sound of Music, My Fair Lady,* and *The Music Man*—Mom's favorites. When I was a little girl, my best friend, Mary, and I were playing hospital with my stuffed animals, and Mary realized that the source of our background music was Mom. She declared, "That was your mom singing? I thought it was someone on the radio. Sandy, your mom is like a professional!" Mom was that good. I loved the sound of her voice and knowing she was happy. Conversely, there was a noticeable void when the singing stopped. I couldn't pinpoint exactly when the change happened, but by the time I was in high school Mom no longer broke out in spontaneous song like she had done when I was a child. Her singing voice had been silenced.

Mom was creative, loved the color blue, and was constantly decorating. Hence our entire house was decorated in shades of blue, except my pink-and-red bedroom and our lavender bathroom. We actually had a purple toilet! My big brother and I would laugh about how Mom held her plastic flower arrangements together with chewed-up cinnamon Dentyne gum, which I think she chewed to hide her smoking breath from Dad. Mom had wanted to be an interior decorator before she dropped out of University of Illinois in her freshman year to marry Dad. Her mother, Grandma Hartman, in some ways ahead of her time, tried to convince Mom to get a degree first, but Mom just wanted to get married; she didn't want to wait to be Dad's wife. Turns out Mom's decision to marry and have children at a young age provided her more time with Ted and me before it all started. I'm so grateful for the time we had.

In the Greek community, Greeks are supposed to marry Greeks, and this was especially true at the time my parents married. No one in Dad's family had ever married a non-Greek. Some of his cousins went to Greece on vacation, picked out a nice Greek girl, and came back married a few weeks later. So Dad was a rebel, pursuing this fair-skinned beauty of mostly German descent, and dating and falling in love before marrying. That just wasn't done in his family. Dad had always been a rebel, and that was one of his best strengths.

Grandma Georgas, Dad's mom, severely disapproved of the marriage. She wouldn't even recognize their Methodist church wedding and insisted that my parents have a second wedding service at the Greek Orthodox church. My non-Greek grandparents also objected. Grandma Hartman warned Mom, "They are not like us. They have a different culture. Are you sure you want to marry him?" It is true that the Greek side of my family

is very different from the non-Greek side. But what Grandma Hartman failed to see was how much closer the Greek side was, as a family, how much more they took care of each other, and how much more fun we had at Greek family gatherings and holiday celebrations when we would dance together at

Mom and Dad on their wedding day with their parents and the bridesmaids, two on the left are Mom's twin sisters.

home, how we would stay close
for our entire lifetimes, and how
we would never grow distant
from each other. I can't say any
of that about my non-Greek side.
Mom was very fortunate to be
welcomed into a family of Greeks.

Both of my grandmothers
have big frowns in the wedding
photos, proudly showing their
disapproval. And my two
grandfathers have huge, wide
grins. But as it turned out, my
Grandma Georgas and Mom
became very close friends.

Eighteen-year-old Mom
as a beautiful bride.

Grandma Georgas spoke well of Mom to her dying day, even
after Mom divorced Dad. And Grandma Hartman loved Dad
and always spoke well of him, too.

Mom and Dad.

Mom and Dad were very
much in love back then. I love to
look at pictures of Dad when he
was young, when he was thin and
had hair—and it wasn't all gray.
He was a cutie, with his dark,
Greek skin and big smile. Mom
and Dad looked good side by side,
Mom an inch taller than 5'6" Dad.

I outgrew both of them by high school.

Dad was the boisterous one.
He had lots of energy. He worked
two jobs for many years, teaching
industrial arts at Fenton High School
in Bensenville, Illinois, and working
as an independent contractor
during evenings, weekends, and
summers. When he was young,
he worked for a developer named
Jay Stream and helped to build

Boisterous Dad.

whole neighborhoods in Carol Stream, Illinois. He also built both houses we lived in; two houses for two of his cousins; a restaurant for two other cousins, the Courtyard in Warrenville; and a vacation home for himself in the mountains of Colorado. His cousin John often used to tell me in his heavy Greek accent, "You daddy have hands of gold." I easily concurred. Dad also made furniture for us, very solid pieces with simple, clean lines, including our dining room set and many coffee and end tables.

One of many Jay Stream homes
Dad built with Jay's Crew.

The first home Dad built, at 1710 North President Street
in Wheaton. We lived here until 1965.

Dad building our second home,
at 907 Ranch Road in Wheaton.

Second home Dad built for us, at 907 Ranch Road in Wheaton

Dad and Ted building our vacation home
in the mountains of Colorado.

Me putting shakes on the Colorado home.

The Colorado house Dad
and Ted built in 1978.

The home Dad built for his cousin John,
at 1613 North President Street in Wheaton.

The home Dad built for his cousin Bill,
at 505 Delles Road in Wheaton.

Courtyard Restaurant, Warrenville, which Dad built
with his partner, Kent Grant, for Dad's cousins Ray and John.

Dad was great at working the crowd at social events, too, and he had a playful sense of humor. However, much of his humor came in the form of cut-down sarcasm, of which I was often the object. Back then, I didn't find that funny at all. Dad never seemed to figure out that when he insulted me that I felt hurt. In his mind, he was giving me love through humor. But sensitive little girls don't feel loved by being ridiculed, even for humor's sake. Now, as an adult, I can understand that Dad's insults are his way of giving me attention and love, and I give it right back to him.

Mom was also a giver. I didn't realize this so much until I went to Greece as an adult and, once again, met relatives who had known Mom years earlier when I was a child. They talked about how Mom had helped them when they came to the U.S., bringing them food and household items. They told me how much Mom had done for their father, Grand Uncle

Dad entertaining us.

George, when he was sick with liver cancer, visiting him and helping him through it all before he went back to Greece to die. They said they still loved her so much, decades after they had last seen her. That really stuck with me, especially because Dad was their blood relative and Mom had divorced him. They said nothing about Dad. They just raved about Mom's kindness.

That same pattern holds for all of Dad's family. His mother, his sister, and all of his cousins who knew Mom talk to this day of how kind and giving she was,

Ted enjoying Dad's humor.

of how they loved her, of how much she did for Dad's cousins when they came from Greece when they lived in the attic of my grandparents' home next door to ours.

I emulate many qualities of both of my parents. People have often told me I have a high level of energy like Dad. Ever since I graduated from college, I have worked a full-time job and have enjoyed hobbies and interests on the side. Mary used to marvel at how I could get so much done in a day. I'm really not sure how I do that. It just happens. I also love to find the funny and get a chuckle out of others, again like Dad. I even studied improvisational acting and comedy at Second City in Chicago, and I'm often coming up with the punch lines, like Dad naturally did. And I love to work the crowd at parties.

As for imitating Mom, I tried to sew, but I decided that it's much more satisfying to just go to the mall. I do love fashion, though, to an expensive fault, and I try to look as nice as I can with my usually-plump build. I also caught Mom's love for singing and music. For years, I performed at restaurants and coffeehouses, and even recorded my own CD. With two entertainers for parents, it's no wonder I became one myself.

My CD Cover.

One last bit of my parents' legacy, for which I am very grateful, is a lack of prejudice. I never heard either of them say anything derogatory about anyone on the basis of their race or ethnicity. Prejudice was so lacking in my home that when I first heard racial comments in high school, I was shocked and appalled. I remember some of the white kids putting down other white kids simply because they were friends with some of the black kids. That was absolutely nonsensical to me, and I couldn't believe anyone could think such stupid things. Boy, was I sheltered! I am so thankful that because of the example of my parents, I didn't have to reprogram my mind about race as an adult. Dad used to say that his father had never said a bad thing about anyone, so I guess Grandpa modeled this for Dad, who in turn modeled it for me. So I did receive many good gifts from my parents, even considering all the bad things that happened.

Performing at a coffeehouse.

Me entertaining others.

Singing for captivated little girls.

Me rockin' at a gig.

Me playing piano as a kid.

1616 Stoddard Avenue in Wheaton, where Mom grew up.

Wheaton High School, where my parent's romance began.

My young Mom all pretty on Easter,
early 1960's.

Me and my big brother on Easter morning, 1962.
I'm 14 months and he is five. I think I want him to leave me alone.

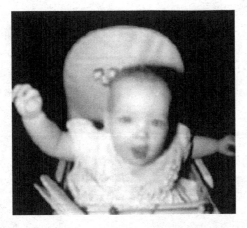

Here I am, hamming it up for the camera as a baby.

Happy young Mom. None of us saw the illness coming.

Right before depression started.

I'm wearing a dress Mom made which matches hers.
I wanted to be just like her.

Pretty white dress
Mom designed and made
to attend my cousin Nicks'
wedding. Mom was an
incredible seamstress.

Red and white checkered dress
Mom made for us.
I still have hers.

My beautiful mother.

Just before Mom started to change.

My pretty mom, very sick with schizophrenia at this time.

Dad's dad, Grandpa Georgas,
leading us in Greek dancing at his home.

I'm the little girl in front of right with my back to the camera.

Dad's brother, Uncle Tom leads. Dad is the shorter man, facing the camera.
To his right is Uncle Gus, Dad's brother-in-law.
This was a typical scene after a big Easter meal.

Great-Uncle George dancing with a chair.

Great-Uncle George (Grandma Georgas's brother)
showing off during our Greek dance.

My family still celebrates with wonderful Greek dancing
we did in my grandparent's home when I was a child.

Chapter 3

FIRST SIGNS

"In about 75% of cases, schizophrenia onset occurs with slowly mounting depressive and negative symptoms that involve increasing functional impairment and cognitive dysfunction." [3]

IN 1970, WHEN I turned ten, my family took a three-week vacation through the West. First we headed from Chicago to good old South Dakota, where we saw the infamous Corn Palace—or as I like to call it, the Corny Palace. I remember driving for two days in our station wagon just to arrive at this large, warehouse-like building inside of which felt like nothing more than an empty gym. Its only feature was a large outdoor mural made of Indian corn. "We came here for this?" I complained, while birds ate the corn and put little holes in the design, which at that time depicted Neil Armstrong taking the first human steps on the moon.

3   Heinz Häfner and Wolfram an der Heiden, "Course and Outcome," in *Clinical Handbook of Schizophrenia*, ed. Kim T. Mueser and Dilip V. Jeste (Guilford 2008), 102.

After the excitement of the Corn Gym, we visited numerous places on our adventure—the Badlands, Mount Rushmore, Yellowstone, Reno, Salt Lake, and Las Vegas, where I have a great memory of being left alone with Ted while Mom and Dad went out to gamble. We

Mom and me floating in Salt Lake.

were staying at a motel that had something like thirty swimming pools scattered across its wide acreage. Ted and I giggled with delight as we searched for and found all thirty pools. It was fun just hanging out with my big brother. Mom and Dad lost a little money gambling, but not enough to cancel the rest of the trip.

We also saw Chinatown, the Golden Gate Bridge, and Fisherman's Wharf in San Francisco, where I remember enjoying a cable car ride and receiving a new Malibu Barbie for my tenth birthday on August 14. It was my first brand-new Barbie.

Golden Gate Bridge in 1970.

From there we ventured to Los Angeles, where we saw Dean Martin driving his convertible right next to our station wagon, causing Mom to blurt out a scream of excitement, and where we were unimpressed by the normal-looking homes of the stars. We also went to Knott's Berry Farm, an amusement park with an Old West theme. I liked it better than Disneyland, which we also visited. And of course, no trip to L.A. would be complete without a visit to Universal Studios, where we watched the parting of the Red Sea.

Next was Hoover Dam, the Grand Canyon, and an Indian reservation in Arizona, where I experienced 110-degree dry heat for the first time. Our last stop was Dallas. We saw

At Disneyland. Ted in the foreground; Mom and me in the car.

where President Kennedy was shot, and we visited Mom's sister Phyllis and her family. Phyllis's young son, Chris, was in the hospital at the time for appendicitis, and I remember waving to him from outside the window: back then, children were not allowed to visit in the hospital. The whole trip was a great experience for which I'm very thankful.

But throughout the vacation something was very wrong. I realized how wrong when Dad showed the sixteen-millimeter movies he had taken along the way. I remember watching the long silent films with my cousins while Dad narrated. In many of the scenes Mom didn't appear with us. That's because for many of the days on the trip she stayed in the hotel room because she didn't feel well. Apparently Dad was not happy about that, and he ridiculed her in front of everyone. As we watched the film, Dad would mock, "Mom isn't shown here because she didn't *feel* good that day." He said it with sarcasm, in a mocking "you were not really sick" tone. I was mad at him for that. First, for not being understanding of his wife, who was ill, and then for publicly ridiculing her for it. It turned out that he never did seem to understand her illness.

That was when schizophrenia first raised its ugly head. On that trip. Mom had withdrawn, often voicing a general "I don't feel well." Just as we all remembered. It continued after the trip, too. It was just a quiet pulling away. It was subtle, but something was wrong. She was thirty-three years old.

It got to the point where Mom didn't bother to get dressed in the morning. She put on her turquoise blue housecoat and lived in it all day. There were times when I saw her on the living room couch just staring into space. Quiet. Absent. That's when I started to lose her.

When Mom's illness persisted so long after the vacation, Dad actually did try to help her. They even traveled to the Mayo Clinic to get answers. Mom said that they had told her she had something called polymyositis, an inflammatory disease that causes fatigue and muscle weakness. Mom lovingly explained to me that her new disease was nothing serious, and I needn't worry. So I didn't. She was still pretty functional and able to be there for me.

Finally one day, Mom suddenly lost it. She called both her

mother and her mother-in-law and told them she was violently ill and had to be taken immediately to the emergency room. Both of my grandmothers complied, although they were very confused about what was wrong with her. Mom demanded that she must go to a better hospital than the suburban ones nearby, so they took her to Loyola Hospital near the city.

Mom loudly told the emergency room doctors that she was sick and needed immediate treatment, and they quickly and correctly assessed the real situation. They took the three ladies to a private room and closed the door, then calmly explained that this was psychosomatic: Mom's illness was all in her head. Mom was fuming. She still believed she was medically ill and needed treatment.

She angrily yelled and made a scene, embarrassing my grandmothers, and commanded them to take her to another hospital. They didn't know what to do except follow her demands. They took her to the next hospital down the road, and the same scene played out again. Mom was dramatic and loud, and again, the doctors told her the same thing.

My grandmothers were stunned. Mom could not be convinced that it wasn't a physical issue, but what was it? After stopping at the two hospitals, they simply brought her home and were left to try to grasp the situation they had just lived through. Grandma Hartman told me that was the first day she saw the illness. Perhaps that was the first day it was finally too big to be denied.

In my junior high years, from 1972 to 1974, Mom's relationship with Dad was increasingly troubled. Mom told me that Dad was a very evil man and a member of the Mafia. That was shocking enough, but then she told me he was having an affair with a woman named Kim. She even drove with me one night to check up on him, to see where he was. He was right where he was supposed to be, but Mom was still convinced he was cheating on her. I wasn't close to Dad, but now Mom convinced me that he really was a bad guy. Believing Mom's delusions, I didn't want anything to do with him.

Next, Mom moved into deep paranoia. She told me that Dad had bugged the phones and that there were cameras in the rooms. It was so disturbing to me that at times I still fear such a thing today. It's terrifying to be thirteen years old and think you are constantly being watched by a secret camera. My home became even more unpleasant and tense.

Then there was the night Mom really freaked out. While Dad was gone for a couple of days to a teacher's convention, she had my brother Ted push heavy furniture in front of the doors. She had him help her hang chains and other noisemaking things from the windows. When I discovered this, I was upset and scared. "What's going on?" I demanded. She told me, "Never mind. Go to your room." But I persisted: "What are you doing? What's going on?" Ted also tried to get me to go away, but I refused. Then Mom revealed the reason for her efforts: "Your father is away tonight, and he is sending men to come hurt me."

"Are they going to hurt me, too?" I fearfully questioned.

"No," she reasoned, "They just want me."

"Are they going to kill you?" I pushed with dread.

"No, they just want to hurt me," Mom answered with a strange calm.

How does she know this? I wondered. *How does she know exactly whom they want to hurt and how badly? Why doesn't she just go to the police or leave, rather than stay home and be a sitting duck?* I was petrified and very confused. I went to my room, closed the door, and hid under my bed. I tightened up in fear.

No men ever came.

Mom later told me even stranger stories about Dad and herself. She said there was a man she used to know from high school—Richard Carlson—whose family owned Carlson paint stores. The Carlsons had been putting fabulous, funny floats in the Wheaton Fourth of July parade for decades. They even put an old-fashioned popcorn cart in the parade every year—one of our pleasant Wheaton traditions.

Mom said that Richard had put that popcorn cart in the parade every year as a secret sign that he still loved her. That was shocking to me, that Mom had some married man out there still carrying a torch for her decades after high school. I even had a class with one of his kids, Linda. Her dad and my mom? Mom had been so happy with Dad before. Had they really drifted so far away from each other?

Mom's stories got stranger. She told me that Dad had set a

fire in the concession stand at a football game at Fenton High School, where Dad worked. He did this, she said, because he knew about Richard's love for her, and Richard put the popcorn cart in the parade every year just for her, so Dad had set the fire in the popcorn maker at the football game to rebel against her and hurt her feelings.

I believed every far-fetched word. I was still very much a child at age thirteen. Children trust what their parents tell them. They take it all as fact. And so I did, no matter how strange it seemed.

When Mom told me in 1974 that she was divorcing Dad, I wasn't shocked. According to her, he was a Mafia man, was having an affair, and was trying to hurt her. Of course, divorce was the right choice! I asked her if I would get to be with her, and she said yes. I felt relieved. Even with all of Mom's bizarre behavior, I still trusted her. I had not been close to Dad and I had withdrawn even more from him because of what Mom told me.

I learned that Dad would get the house and Mom and I would have to move to an apartment. That sucked. I distinctly remember looking out the sliding glass door of the dining room, out into our huge back yard. I thought about all the happy playing I had done in that yard—kick the can, softball games, flashlight tag with the neighbor kids—and about Mary being so close because her yard touched ours. *This is no longer your yard,* I said to myself. And I felt sad. Very sad. I hadn't known I'd lose my home in this, too. But after thinking about it, in a way I understood; Dad had built our house with his own hands and it meant a lot to him to stay there. Still, for me it was a huge loss.

My best friend, Mary, told me that there was a house for sale across the street from hers. "Could your mom buy that house so you can stay in the neighborhood?" Mary pleaded. I asked Mom, and she said no, we were moving to an apartment. But I felt encouraged that it was just a bike ride away and it had a pool.

That summer was the first and, oddly, the only time I witnessed a fight between my parents. They had disagreed from time to time, but Mom never really stood up to Dad until that day. I woke up to hearing them yelling in their bedroom. Their voices were intense, angry, and scary. "You're crazy!" Dad yelled over and over. Mom yelled back something that was muffled through the closed doors. I listened through the walls. Then I heard a thud, a rip, and someone falling. "You ripped my bathrobe!" Mom shouted. More yelling.

Ted and I emerged timidly from our rooms. My brother, then seventeen years old, took the initiative and said, "Let's go." I followed in younger-sister compliance. We took off on our bikes, escaping the painful drama.

As we rode, Ted and I started to argue about Mom. "Mom is crazy, Sandy," Ted insisted. "No she's not!" I defended, and back and forth we debated.

"Sandy, Mom claimed Dad set a fire at a football game to try to hurt her," Ted reasoned.

I explained, "That's because Mom has a secret love, Richard Carlson, and he puts the popcorn cart in the parade every year to show Mom he loves her, and Dad knows that, so he set the fire to get back at her."

Ted stopped his bike. I stopped mine. He paused and looked at me, trying to figure out how to respond. Then he exclaimed loudly, with huge, wide eyes, "That's crazy!"

And that was the first moment I knew. He was right. Mom's story didn't make any sense, and there was something deeply wrong with her. None of us knew what it was, but now, like Dad and Ted, I saw it. It was a turning point for me. I knew that Mom was deeply disturbed. And now, in a different way, so was I.

The divorce went through right around my fourteenth birthday that August. Mom and I moved into a five-story apartment building in nearby Carol Stream. Mary and I biked to and from each other's houses every weekend in warm weather, and got rides from our parents in the cold. We stayed tight. Mom and I did have a pool, and that was fun for me. It was one of the few advantages this new place had to offer. But it turned out that this new home was where I found my greatest gift.

Me in eighth grade.
My parents were divorcing at the time.

I was so groovy in my purple, crushed-velvet get-up.
You can't see the white, lace-up boots I was weraing.
Mom looked fine on the surface, but she was very sick at this time.

Chapter 4

SALVATION

A Child's Divorce Song
(a poem I wrote in high school)

Looked out my window.
Saw my backyard.
I thought for the first time
I think life is hard.

I looked at my mother.
I looked at my dad.
I looked at my brother
and all were sad.

I started to think.
I had to wonder why
things weren't the same anymore
and I started to cry.

What could I do?
Where could I go?
What could I say?
I didn't know.

Little did I know
there was Someone watching over me.

I tried to change my mom.
I tried to change my dad.
I tried to change the whole damn world.
But I was just as bad.

All I had to see
was that Someone was watching over me.

But instead
I just kicked my head
trying to find the answers
to all they said.

Why didn't I see
that Someone was gazing right at me?

Well, finally
I did see.
I saw that He
had love for me.

Well, finally
I looked up and saw Him looking right at me.

Back in 1974, the national divorce rate was climbing, but it wasn't yet a common experience for children. We were the only family in the neighborhood to experience divorce. I remember telling all my neighborhood friends—Mary, the Taylor twins, Carla Stockman, Cheryl Johnson—that I would be moving away because my parents were getting a divorce. Their reaction was surprise and sadness. I appreciated their sympathy, but I also felt like now I was different from everybody else. I felt that now I was a bad kid because I came from a broken home. So I started to rebel.

My rebellion was extremely mild. I just started to swear, which I had never done before. My swearing reflected what I believed about myself: "I came from a broken home, and so I am bad and will be bad."

At the bus stop near our apartment building I met some new girls and we got to be friends. They were Lee Ann Einwalter and Kathy Gildo. We were all freshmen at Wheaton North High School. They, too, were living in apartments with their divorced moms. Wanting to be liked, I thought I could fit in if I showed them that I was a bad kid like them, so I swore a lot around them.

Then they asked me if I wanted to come to a Bible study. The invitation alone changed me for the rest of my life. I realized at that moment that they hadn't rebelled, but instead they were seeking God to help them with life. And so could I. So I did.

Lynda Johnson, who was about ten years older than we three, led the Bible study. She had a huge laugh and a vivacious spirit, and I could see a lot of love in her as well.

One of the first things she had us do was to "write our testimonies." I asked, "What's a testimony?"

"It's how you became a Christian," Kathy jumped in.

I had been raised going to church only twice a year, on Christmas and Easter, to Mom's Methodist church. Mom and Dad hadn't taught me much about God, except how to use his name angrily when you swear. I remember that when I was about ten years old, Mom somehow realized that Ted and I didn't know what the Lord's Prayer was. I hadn't even heard of it. So an old, unused black Bible emerged from the back of a closet, and Mom insisted that Ted and I memorize the Lord's Prayer that instant. I did, and that was it: the entire religious teaching I received from my parents.

But then there was Mary. Mary's family not only went to church, they went twice every Sunday; they went in the morning and then back again in the evening, which I thought was zealous overkill. Mary knew a lot about God and the Bible, and she had been my spiritual mentor, even though she was a year younger. At some point in our many childhood years together, Mary had told me that to be a Christian I had to ask Jesus to come into my heart. And so I did. I don't know when, but I know I did. I also had developed my own habit of praying every night before

I went to bed. I prayed mostly for other people. Also, I used to lose things a lot and would pray and ask God to help me find whatever I was looking for. I remember always finding those lost items and thanking God afterward.

Mary invited me to her Sunday school class from time to time. I loved her class. We sang kid songs instead of those boring old hymns I heard at the Methodist church. We had a lesson that we could understand, and we got to do something artsy that related to the lesson: Wheaton Christian Reformed Church had it right when it came to relating to kids.

Mary's mom wouldn't let Mary bring me every week, though. She feared that my parents would get mad and think that Mary's family was trying to convert me to their Dutch version of Christianity. I wish she had actually talked to Mom about it, because she would have found out that Mom really didn't care one way or the other. After all, it took her ten years to realize that Ted and I didn't know anything about God!

So, by age fourteen I was a Christian, but I had very little knowledge of God. I wrote all of this in my testimony, and after Lynda read it, she knew I was far behind the other girls. So she came to our apartment every week and taught me about God. That's when I heard the gospel for the first time—that is, the central teachings of Christianity. Lynda told me that Jesus had died for our sins. But I was a pretty logical thinker, and this made no sense to me. "Why would he have to die? Why couldn't we just tell God we are sorry for what we do wrong, and that would be enough?" I reasoned. "And what does he have to do with me? He lived 2000 years ago!"

Lynda explained that God is perfect and sinless, and that to be accepted into heaven you can't have any sin. Heaven is a place with no sin, and you must be perfectly sinless because God is holy and sinless and cannot live with sin. The opposite of heaven is death, which is what you get in hell—separation from God for all eternity. Before Jesus walked the earth, God allowed people to be forgiven of their sins by accepting an animal to die in their place. Then they would not have to die when their body dies, but they would live forever and their sins would be forgiven. But this system had some flaws. The people didn't stop sinning, and the sacrifices became ceremonial and were not about true repenting. Plus, a lot of animals got killed!

So God chose to have one sacrifice to pay for all sins of all people. What sacrifice could be valuable enough to pay for such a huge amount of evil? God's one and only Son, who was also God. God sacrificed himself in the form of his only Son. He accepted that sacrifice as punishment for and removal of all sins.

Lynda explained that it's not enough to just know this; we still need to do our own repenting and turning away from sin, and we need to accept Jesus as who he claimed to be—God and man, the one who paid for our sins, the one who allows us to be forgiven and to enter heaven now and for all eternity.

I told Lynda I had already accepted Jesus in my heart as a kid. She suggested that I make a new commitment, because I now had knowledge to go with my faith.

I remember being alone in my little bedroom in that little apartment. I got on my knees and said, "Lord, I really do want to be a Christian. Please forgive all my sins, and come and live in my heart today." Then I expected some kind of sign, like chills up my spine, a wind in the room—something. But nothing happened. So I prayed the same prayer again. Silence. I felt disappointed. It didn't seem like God did anything in reaction to my prayer.

But oh, was I wrong. I couldn't feel it at the moment, but that turning in my heart was deeply significant. God had always been there, but now I was opening myself up to more of him. Something very big shifted in me that day, and I really was different from that point on.

Lynda continued to teach me. Mary's family gave me a Living Bible New Testament; it was the first Bible I read that I actually could understand. I read it, memorized it, and studied it until the pages started to fall out. Then Lynda gave me my first full Bible, a complete Living Bible with Old and New Testaments. I read that one until it nearly disintegrated, too.

Little did I know how much I would need these Bibles and my faith in God to get me through the next few years! As it turned out, they were my salvation in every way.

And he said, "Go out and stand on the mount before the LORD." And behold, the LORD passed by, and a great and strong wind tore the mountains and broke in pieces the rocks before the LORD, but the LORD was not in the wind. And after the wind an earthquake, but the LORD was not in the earthquake. And after the earthquake a fire, but the LORD was not in the fire. And after the fire the sound of a low whisper. And when Elijah heard it, he wrapped his face in his cloak and went out and stood at the entrance of the cave. And behold, there came a voice to him and said, "What are you doing here, Elijah?" (1 Kings 19:11–13, ESV)

Chapter 5

LOSING AND FINDING

*"Parenting capability in individuals with schizophrenia
can range from highly attuned and competent to
adequate, to abusive and/or neglectful." [4]*

ON THE SURFACE, Mom seemed pretty normal when I was
starting high school. She looked nice always, and appeared to
be like any other mom. She was able to present herself so well
that she easily got a job. She did accounting and bookkeeping
for a small company in downtown Wheaton. But home life was
a private living hell.

Mom continued to tell me her delusions: the phones were
bugged; there were cameras in our apartment; her high school
classmate, Richard Carlson, was in love with her; people were
out to get her; a truck tried to hit her one day; someone tried to
poison her another day; she had cancer and only three months
to live—on and on it went. She also talked a lot about the "voices
in her head" that told her all these things.

By that point I knew none of this was true. I spent a lot of
energy trying to convince Mom that she was fearing shadows.
We had lots of arguments as I took on her paranoia and those

---

4   Joanne Nicholson and Laura Miller, "Parenting," in *Clinical Handbook of Schizophrenia*, ed. Kim T. Mueser and Dilip V. Jeste (Guilford 2008), 472.

nasty, unexplained voices. I tried a lot of angles. First I attempted quiet, logical explanations. Then I tried emotional pleas, and finally I screamed in frustration, all to no avail. Often, all I got was her bedroom door slammed in my face. Mom was convinced of her delusions. They were a thick brick wall that could not be penetrated.

Mom was also more and more detached from me. She seemed to be in her own world of thoughts most of the time, somewhere adrift. She didn't seem concerned with the events of my life. She was physically there, but not mentally and emotionally present. My parents had raised me to be independent, and I had to be self-motivated to make sure my homework was done and that I practiced the music my piano teacher assigned. Mom wasn't showing care for my well-being. I felt abandoned emotionally. I felt alone.

I expressed my frustration in a poem I wrote in my early twenties:

I don't understand you
and you don't understand.
Your eyes are odd and
mine hurt me.

Why are you—I must never ask.
I love you, I don't know why.
I can't understand you.
I don't know if you can see me at all.

But I love you as if we were friends.
I'll never understand you,
but maybe you'll understand me,
some day, if you can.

Please, I want to understand you
but you're so queer. I just can't.
I guess no one can really understand anyone else
unless they live the same feelings.

But I can never feel the way you do
and I can never think the way you do
and I don't want to because you scare me.
Really, you do.

Try to explain to me what you are
and try to see things my way.
I want to help you help yourself
but only if you help, too.

One night I screamed so loudly that a neighbor called the police. I was terribly embarrassed when the cop came. Mom explained to the concerned officer that the problem was "teenage rebellion." I remember weeping in front of the uniformed protector, wishing someone would rescue me, even him. No one did.

Many times I got so frustrated with Mom that I would be beside myself. I didn't know what to do. Mom was sick, and no one was helping her. I tried, but everything I did failed. I couldn't help her. I couldn't heal her mind, which meant I was losing her—losing the most important person in my life. Losing the woman who sang to me, held me, nurtured me, and loved me. I watched as her mind drifted away, and a messed up, crazy mind took residence in her beautiful head. She was my only loving, safe family, and now she was fading. It was deeply disturbing to me. Incredibly scary. Overwhelmingly painful. And I dealt with it alone.

After so many frustrating arguments with her, which I always lost, I would go in my room, shut the door, get on my knees, and pour out my heart to God: "God, I can't take this anymore. I can't stand Mom. I can't handle this. It's too much!" Tears fell with the words of my desperate prayers. And in the quiet of my little bedroom, I felt comforted. God soothed me. I experienced God filling my heart with an unexplainable, warm peace.

Each time I retreated into that bedroom, I wanted to stay there for eternity. I needed to escape the insanity. But somehow, in that little sanctuary of prayer, I received a deep peace from God and I would walk out calm, quieted, and kind. After a number of these transformations, Mom began to suggest that

I go in my room when she saw my frustration level rising. Even though she was delusional, she apparently saw the change that took place in me in that little bedroom haven.

On one occasion, as I retreated to my room and wrestled with my pain before God, I told God that I couldn't stand it anymore. The thought that came to me in response was: "Love your mother." Simply that.

I said to God, "I can't. I can't stand her. I can't love her. You will have to help me to love her, God. I can't do it on my own."

And somehow God did: God gave me an ability to love this new, sick person who took over Mom's body, even though I was alone, only fourteen years old, and desperately missed and needed the Mom I used to know. The empowering was miraculous, and it is another reason I believe in God. In that little bedroom temple I encountered him, and I was changed supernaturally by him. That was the most significant way I coped with all the difficulties of her illness.

I also started to create other families to replace the one I had lost, who could help me get through that time. One family was the congregation at Lynda's little church, which I joined. It was a Baptist church of just fifty people. We rented out a little white chapel with a lovely traditional steeple at a Wheaton Christian High School in West Chicago; it is now called Wheaton Academy.

There I met "Aunt Jean," a lovely older woman who became my surrogate aunt. She picked me up on Sundays, along with a few other teens, and brought us to the little church, which had a small youth group of around seven high schoolers. We had many things to bond us: None of our parents went to church, but we were seeking God. We all had parents with problems, too. One girl's parents were alcoholics. Two brothers hinted from time to time that there was physical abuse in their house. We became siblings and friends, and we comforted one another.

I also met a special, very caring man at that church, Reverend Jim Staniels. He had been a pastor, but had to step down when his wife developed severe depression. Eventually he became my emotional dad: he cared a lot about me and seemed to always be there. I loved that church family so much.

Mary was my soul sister, through it all. We saw each other every Saturday at my house. Mom wanted me home on Saturdays because I spent Sundays with Dad, and she didn't want to be alone all weekend.

Mary and I did a lot of normal teen stuff, like attempting to smoke Mom's cigarettes. Boy, did those taste bad! When we thought Mom was coming, we'd quickly throw the cigarettes over the balcony in a panic, only to laugh when we determined that the sound we had heard was just a neighbor in the apartment hallway. But I really didn't want to smoke. I just wanted to try it. I thought it made my breath smell bad, like Kathy Gildo's brother, Alan, who smoked a lot and breathed in our faces as he talked.

Mary's friendship gave me relief. Thank God I had her. She and I would escape for many hours of playing Pac Man at a local arcade called Gala West. At first, the game ate many dollars worth of quarters, but after a while, we got so good that we could play for hours on less than a dollar. A couple of times, after a good long play, Mary even got blisters on her hand. I still

My friend Mary in high school.

love arcades. I turn into that liberated teenager when I take on those playful games.

When it came to Mom, Mary knew better than anyone what I was living through. She and her mom even discussed having me live with them. That was so nice of them. Mary's mom seemed to understand how bad my situation was. But Mary was a year younger than me—just a kid herself. She wasn't able to tell me what to do to deal with it. She had no idea. But she always listened. She was a loving comfort to me, as always. God's love was shown to me through her.

My mom began a pattern that went like this: she got herself a job, worked for awhile, and then quit because, she would declare, "Someone tried to kill me today." I would debate with her, and as usual lose the debate, run to my bedroom, pray in desperation, receive God's peace, and walk out able to face more of life with the craziness. Even with God's peace, I was so concerned for her and for us. Every time, money became an issue when Mom quit her jobs. And her attention to me decreased with each day, as she was just struggling to survive herself.

When I was fifteen, I took a step back, looked at the situation, and said to myself, "Sandy, you are more capable of being an adult and a parent than Mom is. You must take care of yourself, because Mom can't."

So, I got a job so I could make my own money. I made my own food, bought my own clothes, and became even more independent than before. At fifteen, I couldn't get a job at most businesses because by law you had to be sixteen, but I found the DuPage County youth work program, which linked kids to jobs they were eligible for. I got hired to help a lady throw a birthday party for her daughter, complete with a clown, games, and lots of food and fun. I also was hired to baby-sit and do odd jobs.

The month before I became legal to work, I went to every business within walking distance of my apartment and applied for a job. I probably applied at thirty places. McDonald's called. I remember my interview outfit: a striped sweater and brown corduroy pants. That was the nicest outfit I had to wear, even though it was the middle of August. I got hired and started learning the burger business.

Our uniforms were essentially yellow polyester leisure suits. The yellow turned to a permanent gray when grease got on it, so we later switched to brown uniforms, which matched the grease color better. The uniforms actually did more than keep us from ruining our own clothes; they made us all equals. The crew was made up of mostly teens, some of whom came from homes with money and some of whom didn't. But no one knew that at first, because we went to different high schools and wore the equalizing outfits, so we were all free to be friends with one another. I developed another family system with my McDonald's co-workers.

Barb was the girl I got the closest to. A kooky friend who went to a different high school, she lived in one of the little homes Dad had built years before for Jay Stream in Carol Stream—a tiny three-bedroom house that her huge Catholic family squeezed into. Barb told me many years later that she both used and sold drugs in high school, but she never did any of that around me, so

I didn't know about it. We were good friends, plain and simple.

Another special friend was my general manager, Dean, who was in charge of the restaurant. Although Dean was only twenty-five at the time, he seemed much older to me with his salt-and-pepper gray hair. And although he was married, he was a big flirt and flirted often with me, which I loved. It was innocent play, but it meant a lot of positive male attention for me. He essentially showed me that I could attract a man, which is something a teen girl really needs to take in,

Me (left) with co-worker and good friend Terri.

especially one who is shy and overweight, like I was. To this day, I find myself instantly attracted to men with salt-and-pepper gray hair, including my handsome husband.

McDonald's was a second family to me, second to my little church family, that is. People like Barb and Dean listened as I told them about the chaos at home, and they cared. They were in my corner. They were there for me. We all had a great camaraderie.

As an adult, I went back to work for McDonald's: in 2007 I got a job in the computer division at the corporate headquarters in Oak Brook. It was very significant to me to return to McDonald's as a workplace as an adult, even though my adult position is completely different from my teenage job. And to my delight, the comradeship at my office is similar to what I experienced as a teen, although people don't snap wet towels at each other in the corporate office. McDonald's has a way of breeding team spirit among its workforce, both in the stores and in its offices. It did back then, and it still does now.

Behind That Frown

Written when I lived with Mom. I was about 15.

When things are rough
And the chips are down
And I'm really grouchy
And I'm wearing a frown,
Don't be dismayed, Mom.
Please don't be blue.
Behind that frown
I love you.

When I'm uptight.
I take it out on you.
And I start my yelling.
I say I hate you, too.
Don't be dismayed, Mom.
Please don't be blue.
Behind that frown
I love you.

Me at 19, working out my feelings in song.

Chapter 6

THE EVOLUTION

BEFORE MOM AND I moved to our apartment, Mom told me the divorce decree stated that I would have to spend Sundays with Dad. I was not happy about this decision. At that time I just didn't like Dad much. He seemed to always be working and preoccupied with other things. He was often in a bad mood. I didn't know if there were things going on between him and Mom causing this perpetual grouchiness, or if it was from other usual pressures like providing for a family, working two jobs, or some other work stresses. And I had never really spent time alone with him. I complained to Mom, "What am I going to do with my *father* for a *whole day*?" That seemed like a prison sentence. I dreaded the idea, and Mom had no response to console me.

At first those Sundays with Dad were awkward, I think for him as much as for me. Dad planned events to help things along, and Ted came home from college on the weekends to join us. First we went to a ski show, where the latest ski equipment was shown off and for sale. Dad loved skiing and force-fed his sport to all of us. I really didn't care about the ski show, but I was glad that it provided a good way to spend a day together.

On other days we'd do things like go to a movie, like *Airport 1975,* or some other sort of show. When we first began spending Sunday's together, I'd head home right after dinner. I couldn't wait to escape the uncomfortableness. But then things started to change. Soon, I found myself starting to like Dad. He wasn't yelling anymore, as he often had when I was younger. He was broken and hurt.

Before Mom and I moved out, I had seen Dad cry for the first time. I walked past his bedroom to find him lying facedown on his bed, sobbing. I felt bad for him, seeing how hurt he was. Crying was not in Dad's character, but the divorce affected him on a deep level. It melted him. The ice-cold drill sergeant he used to be became a nice guy, or maybe he let himself be who he had always been under his previous intensity and anger. Dad went through a personal transformation, and our relationship changed as a result.

But when my dad first hugged me, I froze completely. My arms were glued at my sides. It was a culture shock for me, and I didn't know how to hug my own father back. So much damage had been done that we hadn't hugged in years. In 1977, I wrote in my journal, "It's so embarrassing—Dad keeps telling me he loves me. I don't know what to say, so I say nothing."

I was afraid Dad's hugs would stop because I had been too frozen to respond with any encouragement. I desperately wanted him to hug me and was so happy that he kept it up, sometimes hugging me heartily and spontaneously at the kitchen table. In time, my hands reached up, and I was able to hug him back. It felt good. Over the years Dad and I would exchange big bear hugs, kisses, and "I love you's" whenever we saw each other, both coming and going.

Our relationship gradually changed so much that eventually Dad didn't have to plan events to pass the time, and Ted didn't have to come home from college to fill the gap. We were able to just be together without it being difficult. I found myself going home later in the evening, as the weeks and months brought healing. Soon I got to the point where I didn't want to go home at all, and I wished I could live with Dad. Although I was losing Mom, I was gaining him, and he was one of the best gifts I could ever have received. I got to the point where I was thankful for the divorce because it caused Dad to change and forced us to spend time together, and we developed such a great closeness as a result. Divorce actually healed us.

Dad also started saying loving things to me all the time. "You're so cute. You are so cute!" was one I heard often. I loved how he gave me the new name of "Sweetie." There is nothing better for a teenage girl than to hear her dad lovingly delight in her. Dad's love healed so much in my heart and melted away so many years of wounds for us both.

He also went to a lot of self-help classes during that time. Several were about handling hard situations without angry outbursts. Dad, who used to yell at a moment's notice and over the stupidest things, transformed into a calm, mellow man whose favorite line was, "That's not terrible. It's just unfortunate." He became safe, and a lot more likeable and loveable as a result. As Dad changed right before my eyes, he taught me that anyone can change themselves, any time. And he continues to be a calm and very likeable guy to this day.

Later in my life, that message would greatly help me overcome the effects of living with my mentally ill mom, which were many.

To Dad

June 16, 1979 (written when I was 18 years old)

Of all the fathers
I could have had
God gave me you
which makes me so very glad.

If God took you away
when I was still small
I really don't think
I'd be here at all.

For you were the one
who spread your arms wide
when I needed someone
to let me inside.

And you were the one
who made my dreams come true.
Those hard to remove dreams
of living with you.

And although I knew I'd be happy
as soon as I walked in your door,
I never dreamed life could be this great
'cause I never had experienced such a life before.

You gave me more love
than I knew how to take.
And you let me know
my move wasn't a mistake.

You advised me and taught me
and you listened well, too.
I wish I wouldn't take for granted
all the things that you do.
Because it hurts me to think
of the life I'd be living
if I didn't have you
and all of your giving.

So I praise God for you
and now, I hope you know why.
I'll love you forever
past the day my body will die.

Chapter 7

ABANDONMENT

*"It is essential to inquire about the presence of children
and to ensure that children under
the care of women with schizophrenia are
being cared for adequately."* [5]

I OFTEN WORKED Saturday night shifts at McDonald's, which was two blocks from our apartment. After the midnight close we'd clean up, which took a good hour. Wired, no one wanted to go home, so we'd usually hang out for another hour, eating some of the unsold burgers and apple pies, goofing off with wet towel fights, and pretending not to notice the married manager who was obviously dating one of the teen girls.

After one of those many Saturday night parties in the red-and-yellow clown-inspired lobby, I walked the two blocks home as usual. When I arrived at our apartment, I discovered that Mom wasn't home, although it was 2:00 a.m.. That was unusual. Mom was strange, but she was home every night.

After nearly three years of living with my erratic mother, nothing fazed me. I figured she was probably just out with one of

---

5   Mary V. Seeman, "Gender," in *Clinical Handbook of Schizophrenia*, ed. Kim T. Mueser and Dilip V. Jeste (New York, Guilford, 2008), 578.

her boyfriends. She had a few, none of them very stable. At that time she was dating a younger guy named Michael who was nice and attractive looking, but he seemed to have a disconnected gaze about him most of the time. I stayed away from that aspect of her life as much as possible. So that night, I just went to bed.

In the morning, Mom's bed was still made and she was nowhere to be found. She hadn't come home at all. Most kids would be alarmed, frightened, or at least angry if their primary and only present parent just disappeared. But by this time, I was so numb to her that I just shrugged it off. I remembered her mentioning something about Florida during the previous week. So I looked for her suitcase to see if maybe she had gone on the Florida trip. I couldn't find the suitcase, but I didn't really know where to look. I got ready for church as usual, made my breakfast as usual, and went on with my independent life as usual. Surprisingly, it felt like just another regular day for me—more living with the insanity.

Aunt Jean picked me up, as usual, to take me to church. During the small and intimate service, Reverend Staniels asked, "Does anyone have a prayer request this morning?" I said in my nonchalant, unaffected tone, "Yeah, I do. I don't know where my mom is." Although I tried to look like I didn't care, I was deeply grateful when I saw the shock on the faces of my church family. They were gravely concerned. They saw through my numb exterior that something was seriously wrong at home. Their reaction felt good to me. Someone cared. And they did pray.

Sunday was the day I visited Dad. Normally Mom would drive me to Dad's, but because she still hadn't returned, I had to call Dad to get a ride. If it had been any other day of the week, I wouldn't have even called him about her absence, but that day I needed a ride from him. When Dad asked why Mom couldn't drive me, I explained, "I don't know where she is. I came home from work late last night and she wasn't here, and she still isn't home. I haven't heard from her." Then Dad said the words I so longed to hear. He declared with determination, "That's it. You've moving in with me."

Dad took charge. He did the adult thing. He acted. He protected me. He took a risk. He had no grounds to have me move in with him because Mom still had official legal custody, but Dad didn't care about that. He did the right thing. My teenage heart was so grateful. Freedom. Escape. No more living with the craziness. And I didn't have to be the one to make the call. Dad did it for me. I was elated.

He came over and I packed. Dad got nervous being in Mom's apartment, afraid she might show up and that there would be an ugly scene. Dad pushed, "Hurry! I don't want her to walk in on this!" So, in about an hour's time, I quickly packed everything I could and moved out.

Mom called me a week later after she returned home. She had gone to Florida with numb-faced Michael. Hadn't even left a note, let alone spending money. Not a single check-in phone call. She had just vanished to go have some fun while her minor child was left at home. Alone.

Mental illness can do that to a good parent. It can make them turn into a very bad one. In my younger years, my sane mother was always there for me—home for lunch when I was a child, making me my favorite sharp cheddar cheese sandwiches. She brought me paper dolls to play with when I was sick. She listened to my daily adventures. She was always there—physically, emotionally, and mentally. This mom in my teen years was just her body with another person living inside, a person who was living with delusions and couldn't hold a job, let alone care for her child. In reality, I didn't have a mom at all. Mom was gone, and not just for a week to the Sunshine State. She was gone for good, or so it seemed at the time.

My young teen mind then realized that having a mentally ill parent is like having an alcoholic parent and a dead parent all in one. Like an alcoholic parent, she can't be trusted. She's sometimes there mentally, but then she leaves, returns, and leaves again, in a sporadic, unpredictable pattern. Most of the time, she's not present. But also it's like losing a parent to death: not only is she gone, but when you ask "Why?" you never get a satisfactory answer. There isn't a good reason. It isn't explainable. It just is. Mom had died, it seemed to me. Although her body was present, she was not there. And there was no explanation for it, really. At least, not for the teenager who still needed her.

Chapter 8

WHY

"Scientists still do not know exactly
what causes schizophrenia." [6]

OF COURSE I'VE wondered for decades what caused Mom's illness. I've read, researched, and also learned by living with and observing Mom. The many studies on schizophrenia have revealed a few things, but still, much about the illness is a mystery. We do know that mothers who contract a serious infection or experience a major emotional trauma during their second trimester of pregnancy have a higher rate of bearing children who later develop schizophrenia.[7] However, most of those moms have perfectly normal babies, so that's not the whole answer. Such events just raise the likelihood. We know that most people with schizophrenia are missing a portion of their brain, perhaps due to an interruption that occurred in their development at some point, although there are people with schizophrenia without this hole, and there are people with this gap who do not have schizophrenia. So again, not a clear

---

6   Ken Duckworth, *Understanding Schizophrenia and Recovery* (Arlington, Va.: National Alliance on Mental Illness, 2008), 4.

7   Michael Foster Green, *Schizophrenia Revealed: From Neurons to Social Interactions* (New York: W. W. Norton, 2001), 32.

determinant, just a hint. Further, "Many neuroscientists believe that one major cause of schizophrenia is excessive dopamine transmission."[8] So, in addition to a brain structure issue, there can be a chemical imbalance.

We know that children of mothers with schizophrenia have a higher likelihood of developing this disease, including when identical twins are adopted by separate families.[9] This shows a genetic component. But again, most children of moms with schizophrenia do not develop the illness themselves.[10] So while genetics play a part, it is not the sole cause. We also know that if one identical twin has schizophrenia, the other one has a 40 to 50 percent chance of also having schizophrenia, while the fraternal twin of someone with schizophrenia has a 10 percent chance of developing the disease.[11] So there is something about genes and the chemistry of the child that seems to contribute to the illness.

People with schizophrenia are also much more likely than others to have been physically abused as children (56.4% versus 3.3% in the general population), and they are much more likely to have experienced childhood sexual abuse (33.6% versus 10.1%.) Likewise, we know that children who experience early emotional neglect, isolation, or other trauma are more likely to have schizophrenia. And 87% of people with schizophrenia have experienced some kind of severe or uncommon trauma in childhood, adulthood, or both. Even more striking, "studies report almost universal (e.g., 98%) exposure to any or all types of trauma over the lifetime" for those with schizophrenia.[12] So we know that abuse and trauma are often key ingredients.

Other studies have shown that certain types of families have higher rates of schizophrenia. Specifically, when family

---

8   Nancy C. Andreasen, *The Broken Brain* (New York: Harper Perennial, 1984), 171.

9   Jonathan Downar and Shitij Kapur, "Biological Theories," in *Clinical Handbook of Schizophrenia*, ed. Kim T. Mueser and Dilip V. Jeste (New York: Guilford, 2008), 27.

10   David J. Castle and Vera Morgan, "Epidemiology," in *Clinical Handbook of Schizophrenia*, ed. Kim T. Mueser and Dilip V. Jeste (New York: Guilford, 2008), 18.

11   Downar and Kapur, "Biological Theories," 27.

12   Stanley D. Rosenberg and Kim T. Mueser, "Trauma and Posttraumatic Stress Syndromes," in *Clinical Handbook of Schizophrenia*, ed. Kim T. Mueser and Dilip V. Jeste (New York: Guilford, 2008), 451.

members are critical, hostile, or overinvolved, schizophrenia is more likely to develop as well as be poorly managed.[13] Further, we know that high stress can be a trigger to the illness.[14]

Then there are other hard-to-explain facts; for example, the disease has far better outcomes in developing countries than in developed countries. So even culture is a mysterious contributor to the ability to live successfully with the illness.[15]

One expert on the condition writes, "The current evidence concerning the causes of schizophrenia is a mosaic. It is quite clear that multiple factors are involved."[16] Another explains:

> Like many other medical illnesses such as cancer or diabetes, schizophrenia seems to be caused by a combination of problems including genetic vulnerability and environmental factors that occur during a person's development. Recent research has identified certain genes that appear to increase risk for schizophrenia. Like cancer and diabetes, the genes only increase the chances of becoming ill; they alone do not cause the illness.[17]

We know that multiple factors seem to cause schizophrenia. One alone doesn't do it, and how each plays into the condition is still unknown. So I don't know what caused Mom's illness, but I have theories.

---

13   Kim T. Mueser and Susan Gingerich, "Illness Self-Management Training," in *Clinical Handbook of Schizophrenia*, ed. Kim T. Mueser and Dilip V. Jeste (New York: Guilford, 2008), 268; Heinz Hafner and Wofram an der Heiden, "Course and Outcome," in *Clinical Handbook of Schizophrenia*, ed. Kim T. Mueser and Dilip V. Jeste (New York: Guilford, 2008), 106; David J. Castle and Vera Morgan "Epidemiology," in Clinical Handbook of Schizophrenia, ed. Kim T. Mueser and Dilip V. Jeste (New York: Guilford, 2008), 22.

14   Paul Bebbington and Elizabeth Kuipers, "Psychosocial Factors," in *Clinical Handbook of Schizophrenia*, ed. Kim T. Mueser and Dilip V. Jeste (New York: Guilford, 2008), 75, 77, 78, 81.

15   Vihang N. Vahia and Ipsit V. Vahia, "Schizophrenia in Developing Countries," in *Clinical Handbook of Schizophrenia*, ed. Kim T. Mueser and Dilip V. Jeste (New York: Guilford, 2008), 551.

16   Andreasen, *Broken Brain*, 222.

17   Randye Kaye, *Ben Behind His Voices: One Family's Journey from the Chaos of Schizophrenia to Hope* (Rowman and Littlefield, 2011), 17.

I think that Mom had some kind of propensity for this disease, either genetically or via her mother's pregnancy issues. Mom was born during the Great Depression, and my grandparents were quite poor. Who knows what kinds of stress Grandma experienced during this first pregnancy? My guess is that Mom had some kind of birth strike against her, which alone didn't cause the illness, but made her much more likely to develop it.

I also know of hints of childhood trauma that my mother experienced. Mom's parents didn't believe in expressing "negative" emotions such as sadness, fear, disappointment, embarrassment, anger, and hurt. These were not allowed in their home. So at best, Mom's family of origin was very dysfunctional.

For instance, Grandpa was extremely moody, and Mom and her sisters spent much of their energy trying to keep their daddy from getting upset so he wouldn't retreat for hours to the basement, abandoning them all. He also liked to drink, and at one point was probably an alcoholic, drinking in that same basement. Grandma told me many times that as a child, Grandpa had been severely beaten by his alcoholic step-dad. So, no doubt Grandpa had unfinished business that affected how he parented.

And Grandma had a thing for enemas. When we were cleaning out her house after she died, my cousin Kim opened her medicine cabinet and found piles of enema kits. We laughed at the absurd discovery, but I knew what these signified. Grandma believed that they were a necessary part of life, so my poor mother had endured many of these embarrassing "cleanings" throughout her childhood and would have been forbidden to express her feelings about them.

Mom actually said to me one day in a rare admission, "It all goes back to when I was six years old and I lost my daddy's love." She was referring to the day when she went from being the only revered child, with all the attention and favor, to being the older sister to two adorable twin girls, Patsy and Phyllis. Twins were quite a novelty back in 1942, before in-vitro fertilization and all of the other baby-making procedures we have today. And Wheaton was a relatively small town back then, making twins even more of a sight to see.

At that time, Mom's family lived in downtown Wheaton, right

next to the train station. All three girls used to play out in the front yard while the commuters walked past. Mom boiled with jealousy as the people stopped to admire the cute little twins, ignoring her.

Mom also got shipped off to her grandmother's house constantly, so her mom could focus on the twins. More rejection. I later witnessed how Grandma habitually raved about the twins and bragged on and on about how great they were, but never praised Mom in the slightest. Her favoritism was obvious, and no doubt deeply wounding to Mom.

Mom with her two beautiful identical twin baby sisters.

I also observed how Grandma would never admit a mistake. She was extremely proud and would twist a story to make herself "right." I remember distinctly one family gathering where someone proved Grandma was wrong about something. She stood frozen, staring into space, trying to come up with a rebuttal— stumped. Speechless. As a kid, I laughed and thought, "Why doesn't she just say, 'Oh, I was mistaken'?" She couldn't. Wouldn't. What a wounded soul she was. Perhaps this was another contributor to the brewing illness in her oldest daughter.

The adorable twins.

Then came Mom's unhappy marriage to Dad. But Mom repressed every bit of her suffering, publicly telling everyone how much she loved Dad. She would say that you could line up all the men in town and let her pick, and she'd always pick Dad. But Dad was often angry, and not the dream man Mom professed him to be. And while Dad certainly didn't cause Mom to be sick, Mom's inability to handle the relationship stress seemed to be another key factor to her illness.

Repression. Freud theorized about a hundred years ago that mental illnesses such as schizophrenia are rooted in some sort of repression of self. While we've learned a lot since Freud, I was very relieved when I learned about his repression theory because of my observations of Mom. I am sure that emotional repression is tied into her illness in some way. My theory is that the human psyche is like a glass bottle. When we don't let ourselves express negative emotions, it is like we are putting black, thick, ugly ooze into the bottle—to hide it. Over time, as we stuff more and more ugly feelings into our glass emotional bottle, we have to cork the top to keep it from exploding, and the pressure in the bottle increases until it is too great for the glass. While "normal" people release the pressure by using their mouths, expressing their feelings in words and tears, people with mental illnesses just hold that cork in tight, and the glass cracks instead. The ugly emotions leak out in bizarre and unnatural ways, and the unpleasant liquid gets everywhere, on everyone. All are shocked and appalled. Many run away, disgusted by the manifestation.

Mom's paranoia was simply her way of releasing negative emotions that she had been taught must never be expressed. After decades of determined repression, they came out through the delusional "cracks."

After I developed this theory, I tested it out with Mom. One day we were in a discount shoe store. Mom was making a little money of her own at the time and decided to buy a pair of five-dollar shoes. Although by this time I was a working adult with plenty of spending money, I knew Mom needed to enjoy the feeling of buying something nice for herself with her own limited funds. So when we got to the cash register, I let Mom buy the shoes herself. But then the cashier announced in a matter-of-fact tone that the shoes were actually seven dollars. Distressed, Mom challenged her: "They were in the five-dollar section!" The uncaring worker stood her ground and insisted, "Someone must have moved them. See, the price tag has seven dollars." I jumped in quickly, "It's OK, Mom. Here's two bucks," and I solved the dilemma. Mom got her much-needed shoes.

Then in the car on the way home, Mom started expressing paranoid fears to me. "My doctor is trying to kill me. He's no good, I tell you. And there's a big conspiracy against me. And,

I have cancer. I'm going to die." On and on she filibustered, in familiar delusional statements.

I wondered what might have triggered her. And then I had my own gleam of understanding. "Mom, are you disappointed because those shoes were seven dollars?"

Mom paused for quite a while. Then she seemed to awaken and declared with anger, "For just once I wanted to be able to buy something for myself with my own money!" And the anger came out, naturally, the way it was meant to be expressed. Her words. And my theory was confirmed and her paranoia temporarily ceased.

After testing it out, I used that technique with her whenever she expressed paranoia. I'd think, "What might be upsetting her? What just happened that triggered her?" After determining the most likely cause, I'd invite Mom to talk about whatever was really bothering her. Time after time, Mom shifted and allowed herself to express her true, bottled-up feelings. I parented her and showed her the way to mental health. To my joy, she came along more times than not. And so I'm convinced that, at least in part, Mom's illness was an abnormal way to express very normal emotions.

What I've also learned is that my discovery about helping Mom express her emotions and reduce paranoia is actually called Cognitive Therapy, which some experts currently consider the only therapy outside of medication that helps people with schizophrenia. In a handbook on schizophrenia, Anthony P. Morrison writes, "Cognitive Therapy has been shown to be superior to other psychological treatments." It is "an effective treatment for persistent psychotic symptoms," and "the effects of Cognitive Therapy are robust over time."[18]

So, I guess I don't get a reward for my discovery, except that I helped Mom heal. I can't think of a better reward. But before I got to this place of understanding, Mom and I first traveled together through some very dark times with her debilitating illness. And in the process, I found healing.

Most people want to run away from those who are mentally

---

18 Anthony P. Morrison, "Cognitive-Behavioral Therapy," in *Clinical Handbook of Schizophrenia*, ed. Kim T. Mueser and Dilip V. Jeste (New York: Guilford Press, 2008), 238.

ill. Many fear these precious souls, unsure of how to respond to them. I have learned to love them, as I learned to love Mom and even help her cope with her illness. And my life is so much richer as a result. Through my journey, I eventually gained Mom back.

Mom's parents, Grandma
and Grandpa Hartman

Chapter 9

LOW POINTS

"Schizophrenia is often associated with significant psychosocial disability, relationship problems, isolation, and lack of gainful employment." [19]

LIVING BACK IN my childhood home—with my old bedroom, in my old neighborhood, with my improved dad—was a dream come true. I was beyond elated. I was overjoyed.

Dad was a stable, steady, and safe adult. He was now there physically and mentally. I knew I could count on him.

That steadiness freed me to focus on my own life, instead of always dealing with Mom's. My grades shot up. I don't remember laboring more over schoolwork, but I found myself easily on the honor roll, with nearly all As. I was more "present" in school. My pay raises at work accelerated, too, going from five-cent-an-hour increases to twenty cents. I was excelling everywhere. And I was happy. Very happy.

Sunday, March 13, 1977 (16 years old)

Today was beautiful. . . . After dinner—which was very good—Ted and I played Frisbee. It was a lot of fun. I

19   David J. Castle and Vera Morgan, "Epidemiology," in *Clinical Handbook of Schizophrenia*, ed. Kim T. Mueser and Dilip V. Jeste (New York, Guilford, 2008), 23.

love Ted, he's neat. Later I called Mary and she told me about her parents and how she stopped an argument. Praise the Lord! I love her, too. I love my dad, too. He attacked me today for fun. He's neat and he cares, too!

One Saturday afternoon about a month after I moved out of Mom's apartment into Dad's house, our doorbell rang and Dad answered the door. I heard a loud and distressed "Sandy!" as Dad called me from the front door. He actually sounded a bit afraid.

I came to the foyer and there were Mom and Dad, standing together at the door. I hadn't seen my parents anywhere near each other for three years, ever since the divorce. So that alone was a shock. Then I saw Mom's condition. She was drunk—*very* drunk. And I had never before seen her drunk in all my sixteen years.

I looked out at the driveway and saw that she had piloted her station wagon right off our driveway, up the grass hill, and onto the flagstone rocks alongside the pavement. She was so drunk she couldn't even stay on the driveway. Another disturbing jolt.

With her very slurred speech Mom asked to move back in with Dad. What a preposterous proposal! She had dumped him and divorced him after nineteen years of marriage, had had no connection with him for three years, was delusional and now very drunk, and thought Dad would possibly take her back? Her mental illness had hit a new low.

Dad told her no with an uncomfortable, fake chuckle. He was pretty good about it, considering how overwhelmed he looked. Feeling it was my job to intercede, I explained, "No, Mom, you can't stay here. You need to go home." And then Mom left, but that wasn't the end of it.

Later that night, a phone call came from the Carol Stream police. "We found your mother," the cop announced in a disgusted tone, "outside by the front of the Baton Rouge apartments, so drunk she was staggering and falling and didn't know where she was. Looks like she wined and dined herself all night long." The officer painted a colorful and shameful scene for my teenage mind to take in. "We took her to Central DuPage Hospital to sober up." I felt ashamed and embarrassed, and kind of mad that the cop was so unsympathetic to both Mom and me. Mom had sunk to an even lower low, and had made herself a spectacle for the entire town to see. But I also felt very sorry for her. She was hurting. Badly.

I called Mary who came over instantly, as always, and cried with me and let me vent. Being a kid herself, she never knew what advice to offer. That made her an excellent listener. She just heard it and wept with me. She gave me so much comfort. I don't know how I would have survived Mom's illness without Mary. She was truly a gift from God.

Tuesday, March 29, 1977

Today is a day I'll NEVER forget. School was nerve-wracking. I have more homework than I've ever had before due to (1) vacation is next week therefore this week is test week, and (2) I am scheduled to work 5 to close tomorrow night. I pray God will help me.

Also, Mom got sickly drunk and is in the hospital tonight sobering up. She'll see a shrink soon. I want to talk to her badly—about Christ. Maybe she'll accept him now.

This is a real test of faith. Things seem to be getting worse and therefore it's harder to keep faith. When I first heard, I cried outrageously. Then I called Mary and she helped me feel better. I love her a lot. God told me not to cry and that Mom will come alive through Christ (he showed me in a verse). Praise Him!

The next day I went to Mom's apartment to get some clothes for her. My journal entry captures the upsetting scene.

Wednesday, March 30, 1977

God—what a horrible day! Praise God! I am scheduled to have 2 tests and a quiz tomorrow (I got out of one) and I couldn't study tonight because I had to work from 5 to midnight!

Praise God I have complete control over myself. I was super-friendly tonight to everyone at work and I didn't cry at all—except when I was alone, and even then I could stop if I wanted to—yeah!

I visited the apartment today. There were 65 cans of beer and 29 bottles of assorted wines—all empty and thrown on the floor—part by the couch, part by her bed on the floor.

She was admitted into a psycho place today. In order for me to see her, her doctor has to approve of me. I'M DYING TO SEE HER! I have to tell her I love her. I have to see her reaction to me   what she thinks of me—and what her mental state is. I HAVE TO! I'm praying.

At this point, my grandparents finally got involved. Grandma called me during the next week and told me that she and Grandpa had put Mom into Alexian Brothers Rehabilitation Center for help with alcoholism. She also emphasized to me how expensive it was and what a financial sacrifice they were making. I thought, *I've already sacrificed three years of my teen years to take care of your daughter while you sat idly by. It's about time you got involved!* I also thought that alcoholism was not her root problem. The real problem was a deep and debilitating mental illness. They were not going to solve that in a few months of alcohol rehab!

Friday, March 18, 1977

Today was better but my heart is not full of joy as it was at the beginning of the week. School was good—I was nice to Becky! Ted didn't bother me.

Work was good—I prayed God would give me the strength to get everyone's order cheerfully and fast—I did! Also, I didn't have to take a taxi home!

Right now I'm wondering what will happen tomorrow when I see Mom. Will she come to know the Lord? Will she completely turn away from him? Will nothing happen? Will she be there?

I desire for her a life with Christ so greatly that I hope tomorrow will be the day she gives in to Jesus. I must say, I doubt God right now but I'll pray tonight with faith. Wondering.

Saturday, March 19, 1977

I called Mom this morning. She didn't answer the phone until I let it ring 5 minutes, then she hung up. I called again. She hung up. I tried once more and I asked her about today and she barely answered. I cried & cried—& cried & cried & prayed. Jesus helped me think straight. I realized that it wouldn't benefit me to go there. The reason I felt I should is because I care about her & I want to help her—But if she doesn't want my help, what can I do? So I decided to wait patiently for her—like God waits for the lost to come to Him.

I may have only been sixteen years old and quite young in my faith, but in many ways I was very adult in much of my thinking by this time, thanks to my single life with my mother. And my conclusions proved to be true. Mom was in Alexian Brothers for a number of months, and then went back to her apartment. But her problems were far from over.

Saturday, April 8, 1977

Today I saw Mom. She said she wants me to move in with her. It was tempting to me. Grandma convinced me it would be wrong for me—she knew because of her childhood. I know she's right because she's lived longer than I. Elders are experienced. I will always listen carefully to what they say.

Saturday, April 16, 1977

Today went fast. I slept until noon and then saw my mom. I realized today that it is going to be quite a task for God to cure her.

After Mom went back to her apartment, she no longer worked, but went to a life skills program offered by the DuPage County Mental Health Department. She lived off of the funds she received in the divorce. Although it was good that Mom was finally getting help for her mental illness, life was still a struggle for her.

One problem with the life skills program was that Mom started to hang out with other severely mentally ill people. However, I didn't mind her new roommate. With her aloof and watery eyes, she was obviously disturbed, but she managed to have a job and was fairly functional.

But then there were the crazy boyfriends. There was one guy who was a good ten years younger than Mom. The three of us decided to go to a movie at Yorktown Cinema. On the way, the song "Just the Way You Are," by Billy Joel, came on the radio, and the nice-looking, odd man started singing the lyrics to me. I started feeling really uncomfortable. Then, during the movie, he started to slowly tickle my side with his finger. I didn't like it, and I squeezed myself into the opposite arm rest. He finally stopped. I couldn't believe my mother's boyfriend had actually made a pass at me. I was incredulous. But that wasn't the worse of it.

After the movie, we all had dinner together at Mom's apartment. The boyfriend asked Mom at the table, "Shall we tell her about our bet?" Mom replied with a giggly "no." He pushed, "Come on, let's tell her." Mom laughed more and said no again. I could sense that this was not going to be good, but my curiosity was raised. "What?" I questioned. The boyfriend ignored Mom's wishes and confessed, "Your mom and I made a bet as to whether or not I could take away your virginity." My jaw dropped. He added, "I bet I could, but your mom bet I couldn't. She won."

"Mom, how could you?" I screamed. I was so angry. I didn't know who she was anymore. The Mom of my childhood would never have done such a violating thing. What was the demon in her body? Where was Mom? What kind of mother bets her boyfriend on whether or not he can take away her daughter's virginity, and then lets him try? My new, crazy Mom, that's who. And unfortunately, I would encounter more of the new, strange and hurtful woman and less of my old, safe Mom during the next few years as we continued to live with the untreated illness of schizophrenia.

"Schizophrenia probably produces more hours and years of suffering than any disease that human beings must bear."[20]

---

20   Nancy C. Andreasen, *The Broken Brain* (New York: Harper Perennial, 1984), 222.

Chapter 10

COLLEGE AND THE TURNING

"The social and economic impact of the disorder on society and families is enormous." [21]

"Women with schizophrenia, compared with women without mental illness, are less likely to have a current partner and have a higher number of lifetime sexual partners." [22]

MY HIGH SCHOOL graduation party consisted of three of my friends and me going out for pizza after the ceremony. That was it. Dad did his best to also be a mom, but he wasn't a party thrower. It was almost a non-event for me.

I decided to go to College of DuPage, the local junior college, for my first two years of college. I had good grades in high school, and certainly could have gone to a more prestigious school, but that didn't matter to me: I liked the idea of living at home with Dad, and having Mary close by, being connected to my church, and still working with my McDonald's family. They all gave me the stability I needed in life.

---

21 Helen Lavretsky, "History of Schizophrenia as a Psychiatric Disorder" in *Clinical Handbook of Schizophrenia*, ed. Kim T. Mueser and Dilip V. Jeste (New York: Guilford, 2008), 3.

22 Joanne Nicholson and Laura Miller, "Parenting," in *Clinical Handbook of Schizophrenia*, ed. Kim T. Mueser and Dilip V. Jeste (New York: Guilford, 2008), 471.

I had three majors floating in my head at that time—engineering, computer science, and psychology. So I took engineering prep classes— calculus, chemistry, and physics—as well as computer programming classes and Psychology 100. In my psych class I met a psychiatrist for the first time: my teacher. I found the class to be kind of boring, but I wanted to talk to him about how to help Mom.

He was kind enough to meet with me, and I told him about Mom and asked him, "How can I help her be well?"

He responded, "What makes you think your mom *wants* to be well?"

"Of course she wants to be well. Everyone does," I insisted.

He countered, "If she wants to change, she will. She might be more content with herself than you realize."

Although at first I was not happy with his reply, after a good ponder I realized that it did make some sense. His point was that you really can't change another person: they have to want to change themselves—a classic Psych 100 lesson.

My teacher's words helped me to let go of some of my need to fix Mom, but there was much more work to be done on that. I decided I really didn't want to major in psychology. I ended up choosing computer science because in one of the classes, I had to write calculus equations in Fortran computer program code, and it was the most fun of all my college courses. So I decided to do programming for a living, and I hoped to be a scientific programmer eventually. I achieved this goal after I graduated with a bachelor's degree in computer science from Northern Illinois University, and I took a job in which I wrote programs for the engineering division of a natural gas pipeline company. It proved to be all I had hoped for in a job and a career.

But those college years were not without more Mom drama. In fact, they were some of her worst years.

Who You Used to Be

You remind me of who you used to be.
Do you remember? I do so clearly.
You used to laugh. Now you do infrequently
but when you do, your face flashes before me.
Then I remember your smile and the look of love in
        your eyes.
But now they're hollow and full of unanswered "whys".
I miss you. Oh, I miss you
and yet you're right here in front of me.
I wish I could reach inside you and lead you out
but you're locked in thick iron and I've tried every key.
If you ever wake up from this mesmerizing sleep
I will still be here to love you
and be yours, forever yours, forever to keep.

Mom's boyfriends continued to be awful. There was one older man who treated the cat so badly that the little long-haired tan tabby changed from a sweet, kind and gentle little kitty to an aggressive killer, practically ripping my hand off when I tried to pet it. What did he do to that poor cat to make it so mean? That boyfriend was later arrested for wearing Mom's bathing suit and one of her wigs while prancing outside at the apartment community pool.

There was the time when I still lived with Mom, and I'd answered the phone and a man asked for her. When I told him she wasn't there, he said, "Do you want to sip my cock?" I slammed down the phone as fast as I could and screamed with disgust.

Then Mom let Bill move in. Bill was a slightly pudgy, brown-haired plain-looking guy who was a few years younger than Mom. Bill loved to gamble. At first he was exciting for Mom, taking her to the track and to off-track-betting locations. She had a lot of fun. Bill had many good times gambling away Mom's money, and because her paranoia kept her from working, and my child support payments stopped after I moved out, she had very little to live on. Mom passively gave it all to Bill, believing his "I'll make money for us" bull. Funny, he never was able to earn a living at the track.

That's when Mom deteriorated into depression.

Bill treated her cruelly. She complained to me that he would make her sit in the bathtub naked and in cold water until she practically froze. How did he make her do that? Did he beat her? Was Mom so passive that she wouldn't just stand up to him and kick him out? She never told me many details, but my impression of Bill was that he was a physical abuser and Mom felt helpless to stand up to him. This time, instead of standing up for herself, she decided to die by jumping off her fourth-floor balcony. She had no money, she felt powerless against this mean man, I was gone, and Dad wouldn't take her back, so she wanted to end it all.

Mom tried to jump to the ground, but got caught on a pointy part of the wrought-iron railing one floor beneath her balcony. The railing speared her upper arm near the shoulder. I can't imagine the pain, both the intense physical pain to her body and the deep emotional pain she must have been in to have done this.

Someone called the fire department, and emergency responders got Mom down and took her to be treated. Her arm was not broken, but it required hundreds of stitches.

After being sewn back together, Mom was taken to her first mental institution, Madden, in Maywood. I was nineteen years old. When I first visited her there, I could see the depression engulfing her. It hurt me, too. It hurt to see her so sad. There was little conversation. I was just there with her.

Her caseworker at the time asked to meet with my brother Ted and me. The caseworker was the one who finally gave us a label for Mom's illness—paranoid schizophrenia. I felt so relieved to finally hear a diagnosis. It validated the previous nine years of hell. Yes, Mom has a serious and debilitating disease of the brain. This isn't her choice. It took her over. She is the victim of it, not the cause of it.

Then the caseworker explained that they were forced to release Mom because she had been admitted on her own free will, and now she was demanding to leave. She explained that Mom's boyfriend Bill had come to visit and had promised to marry Mom, so now Mom wanted to leave. Later I learned from neighbors that while Mom was hospitalized, Bill had been having other women over to her apartment.

The caseworker said that they didn't think Mom should leave, that she was still depressed and she was not safe, but that there was nothing they could legally do to stop her.

My heart sank. Just like me and Mom, the hospital was powerless against this illness.

And so they released her. Mom went home. Bill never married her, but he gambled away her last penny. The rent hadn't been paid in months. There was no money for food. A few months after she was released, Mom jumped off the balcony again. This time she hit earth. And so ended a tumultuous era of Mom's life; her life of independence ceased on that day. But mercifully, a new life of recovery began.

Please Live, for Me

You're my friend. I love you, you know.
But I cry when I think of you,
        though I never let it show.
'Cause I know you're unhappy
and you really want to die
        but I need you, in a way,
        so give life another try.
It won't be easy, it never is though,
and at times, you'll get mad,
        when life gets hard,
        like a strong damaging blow.
But, you see, your life is important.
You're a specific human being.
        It's not like you're insignificant
        or that your life doesn't mean a thing.
I need you in this world
to do what a mother does;
        to think as a mother thinks;
        to love as a mother loves.
Please Live, for Me

Chapter 11

MOVEMENT

"The single largest cause of excessive mortality in schizophrenia is suicide, with suicide rates elevated above not only population rates but also rates for other psychiatric disorders." [23]

AFTER MOM'S INJURY was treated at Central DuPage Hospital, she was moved to the medical wing of the Elgin State Mental Hospital. I visited her weekly, facing the painful reality of the situation head-on. Mom walked with slow, difficult steps, guided by her new walker, while her broken hip, legs, and ribs healed from the attempted-suicide leap. Her depression was shockingly thick. She was barely responsive as I filled the air with small details of my college life.

In a central location on her floor there was an old wooden upright piano. I encouraged Mom to make the short trip to the area, then played for her some classical pieces I'd memorized, giving Mom a private concert using the talent she had made sure I developed thanks to all those years of piano lessons. Mom just silently listened, still and motionless.

After a few songs, another older woman slowly emerged from around a corner, pulling herself in her wheelchair with

---

23   David J. Castle and Vera Morgan, "Epidemiology," in *Clinical Handbook of Schizophrenia*, ed. Kim T. Mueser and Dilip V. Jeste (New York: Guilford, 2008), 21.

her feet. She had a smile on her face, and she looked right into my eyes and said, "Play." She was another wounded soul, and it encouraged me that my fingers were massaging her hurting heart with the beautiful notes. It was then that I learned, once again, the power of music. Music can soothe, and it can even heal. I was so glad I could give Mom something to comfort her and perhaps lift her, at least a little, out of the deep despair she was stuck in at that time.

Eventually Mom's bones healed enough for her to walk on her own, and she was allowed to leave the mental hospital for outings with me. She was still severely depressed and barely spoke. When she did break her silence, she erupted in long ramblings filled with both paranoid phobias and complaints about how bad her life was. At first I was upset at the deep negativity, but then I realized that at least she was talking and getting out some of the pain. So I just listened. I had learned to validate her emotions under the words and just love her as she was.

Elgin was not a long-term facility, and the staff there worked to guide Mom to a place of mental stability, at least enough to allow her to leave. Finally Mom pulled out of that depression, but she was still fighting her many uncontrollable delusions.

While she was in the state hospital, she wrote me several letters:

September 6, 1980

Dear Sandy,
I am once again a prisoner in Elgin.

October 16, 1980

Dear Sandy,
It was so delightful to talk to you, if only for 2 minutes. I got your letter too, and am glad to hear you are doing so well in school.
Please take care of yourself so that you don't have so many colds. You had them for the past six years—what a drag.
I have developed a lump on my left arm, and thank God that surgeon I saw yesterday refused

to operate on it. I have been blithered twice in surgery and will have no more operations.

Last week I was taken to an ear doctor who tried to rupture my eardrum. Very funny.

You would have made a lovely homecoming queen dear.

January 30, 1981

Dear Sandy,

As you can see by my return address I am in Elgin. Today is the first day I didn't wake up homicidal or suicidal in 3 weeks.

They have me on suicide precautions and I had to sleep out in the hall by the aides' station. I can get along on no sleep now—I was up all night 3 nights.

October 20, 1981

Dear Sandra,

Things in Elgin funny farm haven't been going too well since your visit. I was out of my head for 3 days, have been awake since 3:30 and missed work yesterday. Thank you so much for visiting and the shopping trip. I love the purse.

October 29, 1981

Dear Sandra,

I was very impressed with your knowledge of the Bible and I enjoyed your sermon. I have been going to Bible Study here on the Ward once a week and enjoy it immensely.

I have been having counseling sessions on Wednesday and Friday mornings with my counselor, Kim Bimbo, and Dennis Dee, head of Unit ATC 6&8. They are either going to discharge me or send me to extended care in 30 days.

Please say a prayer that I get discharged—those extended care Wards are really discouraging to be kept on.

I missed 3 days of workshop due to crazy in the head—we have germ warfare here—a good friend of mine named Frank died yesterday of heart failure—he was only 67 years old. I feel bad about it.

February 8, 1982

Dear Sandy,

I am being transferred to Kilborne tomorrow. It is straight down the street from 6&8. Kilborne is a long-term ward. I am waiting to pack this afternoon.

My other news is that I start workshop next Tuesday, the 16th.

I haven't heard from you for so long, please write when you are coming home and I will try to get a pass.

I have no idea what life on Kilborne will be like and I am scared to go. They will be happy on 6&8 to get rid of me tho.

Haven't heard from Grandma H either.

Love,
Mom

August 30, 1982

Dear Sandra,

Well as you can see by the return envelope I am back in Elgin by self request. I tried suicide with a bottle of aspirin the day after you took me to see "An Officer and a Gentleman." They knew, of course. And gave me an antidote in my pills that night. I stared into space and vomited until 2 A.M. Boy that was a dumb thing to do— my head was ringing for days after.

Then I got the brilliant idea of moving back to Elgin on Oct 1 and renting a room at the Elgin Inn. After I made the room reservation I became suicidal 2 days in a row and decided I had better come back. When I arrived Saturday night I was no longer suicidal because I threw up the poison hot dog!

I am under close observation and don't have a pass. If you still want to come and see me Saturday or Sunday I would be delighted.

Thank you for the sweet card, dear.

Love,
Mom

October 4, 1982

Dear Sandy,

I enjoyed your visit very much—the movie and hamburger were lots of fun.

My life here on the ward is about the same.

There is yelling and fighting here all the time. Even Delores beat up 2 girls one morning.

October 20, 1982

Dear Sandra,

I hope you are having a ball in Houston and don't have to work so hard. Can you visit me on Sunday Oct 31? We should celebrate my birthday—I will be 46. I wish I could see Ted on his birthday, too.

Please bring my black winter coat, my boots, my size 16 black pants and a needle with a big eye.

Speaking of eyes, we had a real tragedy here 2 nights ago. A young girl named Patty ran away during the day. Two off-duty security officers picked her up in Elgin running in traffic. I thought she was dead when they brought her

back—she just lay on the floor. Then after supper
she was dressed in a hospital gown and the Dr.
from M&S saw her. About 8:20 she poked one of
her eyes out. They were all shook up here until
the ambulance arrived. She is in St. Joseph's
hospital with around-the-clock surveillance
from our staff.

We had entered a new phase in our journey, the "Where do we put Mom?" dilemma. There were many attempts at finding satisfactory living quarters for Mom—so many, I'm not sure if I remember them all.

One place the staff in Elgin placed her was a halfway house, the Commodore Inn, in what looked to me to be a not-so-good neighborhood on the West Side of Chicago. I was pretty sure Mom's roommate was an ex-con, and I was very worried for Mom's safety. Mother hated that place and told the management there that she was going to kill herself. Not wanting a suicide on their hands, they quickly shipped Mom back to Elgin for safekeeping.

When I visited Mom in Elgin during her second stay, she told me that's where she wanted to remain. She had actually started to like the mental institution better than the outside world. Elgin also had a work program, which allowed her to make a little money as well as keep busy. She described her job as putting together "blow pipes." I never fully understood what that was, or why it would be a job, but Mom liked the easy, mindless work and small but encouraging pay.

After a few months, the staff at Elgin decided to give Mom another try at relative freedom. This time they placed her in a nursing home in a far north suburb of Chicago, Bayside Terrace in Waukegan. It was a much nicer place than the Commodore Inn, and although I didn't like the hour-long drive to get there, I thought it was many notches above the seedy halfway house in Chicago.

One Saturday when I visited, I brought my guitar and sang a set of sweet love songs for my young mom and the old people who surrounded her in the home. Mom loved the music, and it seemed to lift her spirits. After the set, a white-haired, thin old man shuffled up to me in small, slow steps, saying nothing but breathing heavily and smacking his lips along the way. He reached deep into his pocket and pulled out a quarter, pushed it down hard into my palm, then, saying nothing, turned and slowly shuffled away. Once again, I saw the power of music. I also knew that that little twenty-five cents was a huge thank you from the wordless man. I kept that quarter for decades as a monument to that touching moment.

Mom still wasn't happy in the suburban home. She longed for the safe haven of Elgin, along with the work program they had. So she told the nurses she was going to kill herself so she could get her free ticket back to Elgin. Mom wasn't suicidal during that time, she was just unsettled.

Just like the halfway house, the nursing home fell for it and shipped her back to her favorite mental institution. Like a devoted groupie, I visited Mom often in Elgin, as I did wherever she went. Sometimes I would bring my guitar and sing for Mom and the other patients. I would watch these despondent women awake from their motionless stares as I started to strum my guitar and sing my songs. Music awoke the lost ladies and enabled them to be alive for a little while. I was amazed at the powerful change brought on by song.

It was very interesting and educational to chat with these locked-up women after I finished my sets. One young, pretty blonde girl who looked younger than I was came up and asked me in a whispery voice, "Do you have any heroin?" Sheltered as I was, I was shocked by the question and awkwardly said, "No, honey. Don't you know that stuff isn't good for you?"

Another woman came up and, at an impressively fast pace, disclosed her life story to me as I packed up my guitar. She followed me to the door, sharing details the entire time.

There was one dear moment I will never forget. One of the women gave me a small metal cross after I had sung a few songs. It was her cross, her comfort, and she wanted me to have it. I told her, "No, you should keep that," but she insisted that she wanted me to have it. And in this closed ward of a hardcore mental institution, I saw a loving and beautiful heart in this sweet woman. So

I accepted the cross and have carried it with me ever since. It continually reminds me of the powerful connection of music.

In fact, that little cross carries an even larger weight of meaning for me. It holds the truth that love and hope can exist anywhere, for anyone, if we choose it, just as that beautiful giver showed. It reminds me of the transforming power not only of music, but of the love of God. Thick walls of delusion can be penetrated by music, love, and God.

The lesson of the little cross has been a central brick in the foundation of my life. It has allowed me a special ability to overcome and heal from the years of turmoil with Mom. I think that in many ways the message of that cross also brought healing to my unstable mother, a fact that became evident in our next few years together.

Mom's many homes, 1979–1983

Date moved to location	Location's name	City
Sometime in 1979	Elgin State Mental Hospital	Elgin
Around 1980	Convent of St. Anne	Chicago
September 1, 1980	Elgin State Mental Hospital	Elgin
December 28, 1980	The Commodore Inn	Chicago
January 18, 1981	Elgin State Mental Hospital	Elgin
March 28, 1981	Bayside Terrace	Waukegan
September 6, 1981	Elgin State Mental Hospital	Elgin
May 3, 1982	Grasmere Residential Hotel	Chicago
May 12, 1982	Elgin State Mental Hospital	Elgin
August 1, 1982	Skokie Meadows	Skokie
August 30, 1982	Elgin State Mental Hospital	Elgin
May 25, 1983	Countryside Healthcare Center	Aurora

The Mental Institution
(I wrote this when Mom was in Elgin State Mental Hospital)

The snow blankets the scenic park;
caged with ancient iron railing;
black and detailed;
a meek barrier.

Scarce footprints
never to be seen for
no one is out.

The domed, large building
looks like a vacant government building.

Red bars and broken glass
dress the windows bare.

The circle drive
used to have grass between the cracks
but now, white and still.

The building is lifeless
yet it haunts,
for people live here.

The streets,
lined with sparse parked cars,
dare not have people walking.

Every building, repetitious,
bare and vacant,
yet, people are alive inside.

The scene is still,
dead,
no where,
but, there are people somewhere
living.

Their hearts beat,
their lungs breathe.
They move. They can even think.

But they are hidden,
locked away.
Never to be free.

Inside,
the floors are stained with filth
although mopped daily.

Soap, ammonia, more dirt.

The walls, blurred beige;
no importance.

Yet, they hold in
and they hold up.
Without them
all would crumble.

The air
smells of its own scent;
unique to the building and
the inhabitants inside.

The people,
part of the human race,
part of humanity,
yet forgotten,
put aside, away,
labeled, stamped, and outcast.

I am sick.
They are people.
They have lives.

Yes, they are noticeably different
but they are also noticeably the same.
But who cares enough to see that?
Who can love those who are different?

God does.
He never forgets them,
I will never forget them.

It's not just a nice park:
It's a home.
As long as there are people alive, they matter.

If I matter
why shouldn't they?
Just because they're sick—
it's not like they're infected,
contagious or something.

Put them away.
Lock them up.
Forget them,
but don't kill them.
Just take the world from them.

It's crazy!
It's neurotic!
The whole world is neurotic!
Yet those who are sick are
labeled neurotic.

I hate the hypocrisy!
They shouldn't have the pressures we have
but they shouldn't be forgotten!
Outcasts!
Like lepers, or the plague.

They are humans!
They are humans!

Don't label them anything else!
It's not fair and
it's not right.

Anyone in need is your neighbor.
These people need people to care.
Love your neighbor as yourself.
That includes these people
who are forgotten,
rejected,
laughed at,
labeled. Labeled!
"Crazy people!"
I am sick.

They are just humans.
What crime is in that?
Just because one cannot understand them
doesn't mean they can call them names.

They are people.
Locked in solitude.
In still buildings,
vacant, lifeless,
yet,
filled with life.

Chapter 12

THE CONVENT AND THE CRAZY

*"Homelessness and housing instability are
common in people with schizophrenia."* [24]

AFTER MORE ATTEMPTS to find a good home for Mom, Elgin State Mental Hospital finally got it right. She was moved to a convent on the far north side of Chicago. Mom had her own private room down a long hall on the third floor of a large, red brick building, far away from where the nuns stayed. And she had a job that suited her well—hand-mending clothes for the nuns. Mom was always great with a needle and thread, so this was an ideal situation. Mom had freedom to go out, and all meals were provided for her. The grounds were spacious, well-kept, and lovely. I was so happy Mom finally had a good home.

Mom liked the place and stayed there nearly a year, which was a long stint for this unstable, discontented woman. But Mom was lonely for companionship, and not the kind celibate nuns could provide. So on Saturday nights Mom went out for a good time, enjoying cocktails and the intimate company of men. I don't know how the nuns eventually discovered Mom's not-

---

24   Alan Felix, Dan Herman, and Ezra Susser, "Housing Instability and Homelessness," in *Clinical Handbook of Schizophrenia*, ed. Kim T. Mueser and Dilip V. Jeste (New York: Guilford, 2008), 422.

so-holy ways, but it was unacceptable behavior and once again, Mom was shipped back to Elgin, this time not by her choice.

I had graduated from college, was working as a scientific computer programmer, and was living back home with Dad while paying for the silver Toyota Celica I had bought entirely on credit as a graduation present to myself. My little high school church of fifty had dwindled down to only five members, so we voted to dissolve our congregation. Aunt Jean and I church-shopped together and ended up at a similar, 200-person church: the First Baptist Church of Glen Ellyn. My church family was new and larger in size, but just as connected and caring as the small church of my adolescence.

Elgin made another attempt at moving Mom out. This time they placed her in a nursing home on the west side of Aurora, a far western suburb. I was scared. I wondered: Will Mom stay? Will she hate it? Will she get in trouble there?

One Sunday night I went to First Baptist's intimate evening service. At one point the pastor asked, "Does anyone have any prayer requests tonight?" I raised my hand, which was very rare for me. After his invitation to share, I said, "I need you to pray for my mom. She has lived in a lot of places in the last few years and she has had a very difficult time adjusting to each and never stays anywhere for long. Can you pray that she accepts this place and stays there?"

And they prayed.

About a week later I visited Mom, as usual. The nursing home was clean and decorated very nicely, and it looked good to me. Mom and I sat together on her bed in her two-person room. "How do you like it?" I asked. To my great disappointment she complained, "I hate it. It's no good. The nurses are terrible. The doctor doesn't know what he's doing. He's trying to kill me. And I'm sick, I have cancer." On and on she filibustered with her paranoid negativity.

Then a rare event happened for me. I burst into heavy tears. Rare tears. Needed tears. I realized that Mom was not happy and that the turmoil would continue. It wasn't going to end. I was sentenced for life to continuing worry and anxiety over this lady who used to give me so much love. Years of tears flowed onto her blue flowered bedspread.

Then a miracle occurred. Mom became a mother again, just long enough to help me through. She finally saw the toll her life was taking on me, and out of her old motherly love for me, she stepped out of her illness long enough to comfort me. She said, "Sandy, it's not that bad. I didn't say I would die."

I then blurted through my heavy tears, "I just wish you'd stay somewhere. I can't stand it anymore, Mom. I'm worried about you, and I just want you to stay in one place and be happy."

That was 1983. Mom still lives in that home today. God answered my prayer in a huge way. I think God did so in equal measure by freeing me to cry and by awakening Mom long enough for her to listen and, on some level, understand. That moment, that day, was one of the most healing moments of both of our lives. And more healing flowed after that.

I Love You, Mom
Mother's Day, 1984

Of all the poems and songs and rhymes
that have been written for this day
none of their beautiful verses
truly express what I want to say.

No, I don't have any wise or profound wisdom,
Nor can I really say anything new.
My simple message of this day
is Mom—I love you!

Chapter 13

THE BREAKUP

*"Children whose parents have schizophrenia may
be pressed into service as caretakers of ill parents,
or of siblings. Some children whose parents have
schizophrenia suggest that this role reversal enhanced
their coping and caregiving skills; others report having
suffered from age-inappropriate family burdens."* [25]

Learning to Let You Go

(A song about how I had spent the various stages of my life
learning to let go of Mom, written July 10, 1997)

1. I took my first few steps
    holding tightly to your hand.
    I screamed with delight
    when I finally could stand.
        Knowing you were close
        was my strong security.
        Free to explore
        and free to be.
    I was

---

[25] Joanne Nicolson and Laura Miller, "Parenting," in *Clinical Handbook of Schizophrenia*, ed. Kim T. Mueser and Dilip V. Jeste (New York: Guilford, 2008), 473.

> Learning to let you go. Oh, yeah.
> Learning to let you go.

2. Fights about my clothes
   and my independent ways
   seemed my theme as a teen;
   never feeling quite OK.
> You gave me lots of room
> to find out who I was.
> I know you understood.
> You knew it was because

I was
> Learning to let you go. Oh, yeah.
> Learning to let you go.

3. Now in my grown-up years,
   I find I'm often the mom.
   I help your memory.
   I keep you safe and calm.
> As I remember
> your letting me be me,
> I also let you go.
> I know I can let you be.

So I'm
> Learning to let you go. Oh, yeah.
> Learning to let you go.

Having journeyed through the instability and scare of mental illness with Mom naturally had a huge impact on who I was and how I lived. While other twenty-something girls were working on finding a man and starting a family, I was focused on helping Mom. I would always visit her every other Saturday, driving her wherever she wanted to go, buying for her anything she wanted, then making her my Saturday night date as well, usually dining at her favorite restaurant, Ponderosa. I remember one Saturday when I drove her to four different KMarts to try to find one particular type of shoe she wanted, and to no avail. I continued to do everything I could to make her happy, not spending energy on my own life.

At that time, Mom's parents had pulled away and never visited her, although they were good about writing her. Ted visited on occasion, but I was her only regular and frequent family contact. I learned later that their response is fairly common. The family, overwhelmed by the illness, avoids it and the person with it: the pain is so great. Plus, in Mom's family, negative emotions were forbidden. So the family didn't allow her to be too close because she would bring with her a boatload of pain for them, which they didn't have the life skills to handle.

Both of Mom's sisters had married men whom they would later divorce, and one husband was shockingly abusive: my aunts clearly had their own difficulties and challenges to handle. And so I felt I was the only one left to help Mom. I felt responsible. I loved her and would not abandon her. I'd rather abandon myself. And essentially, that's what I did.

I learned a lot from an older lady I worked with, Kristi. She was pretty, thin, and blond, and had a cutting tongue. She was raging mad at her father and brother who had both sexually abused her when she was a child, and she was also angry about her brother having schizophrenia and being homeless. She took her pain out on all of us.

But surprisingly, Kristi did more for me than any person I had ever worked with. She told me I was codependent and that it wasn't good. A codependent, according to Melody Beattie, author of the famous book *Codependent No More*, is a person "who has let another person's behavior affect him or her, and who is obsessed with controlling that person's behavior."[26] Kristi helped me to see that I was too obsessed with Mom and that I wasn't helping her. Instead, I was the one who needed to change. Although I hated Kristi's scolding tone, I knew there was some solid truth to her cutting words. I was slightly enlightened after reading the famous book myself, but this was just the beginning.

In the summer of that year, Kristi lent me an extensive video series called "John Bradshaw on the Family," which she had recorded off a public TV station during the annual fundraising telethon. On Friday night of the three-day Labor Day weekend, I sat down and watched the first video of the series. In it, John

---

26 Melody Beattie, *Codependent No More* (Center City, Minn.: Hazelden Foundation, 1992), 36.

Bradshaw logically explained that when there is a parent who essentially "steps out" because of alcoholism, death, or mental illness, the rest of the family changes and responds to make up for the loss and to fill in the gaps. The children tend to take on roles: there's the Responsible One, who takes over the parenting; the Hero, who works to give the family much-needed dignity; the Lost One, who becomes quiet and unnoticed to try to keep the peace; or the Caretaker, who works to fill the void of missing warmth in the family. Other roles are the Perfect One, the Always Being Helpful One, the Rebel, the Enabler, and the Surrogate Spouse. I realized that I was most definitely the Responsible One because I felt like I was the only one who could care for Mom.

I watched the entire series that weekend and was truly changed by the insightful wisdom. I saw that I indeed needed to heal. It wasn't just Mom who was sick. I was too.

Dad had moved on in his life and had found an amazing woman who was absolutely perfect for him. That November they married. Although I was elated that Dad had found love again and now had this terrific partner, the week before the ceremony I found myself bursting into tears in the silence of my apartment. I was crying over the obvious reality that my parents would never be married to each other again. I was a twenty-nine-year-old adult, my parents had divorced fifteen years earlier and had barely spoken since, and Mom had been a suicidal alcoholic and still lived with schizophrenia. But I found that somewhere in my little-girl heart I still hoped for my mommy and daddy to love each other again. Emotional pain is universes away from logical reality. It was the first time I allowed myself to grieve for my parents' divorce—fifteen years after the event. I had been too busy trying to heal Mom to feel my own pain. But now I let myself cry.

Those unplanned tears helped me realize that I needed some help getting through this hurt. Angry but wise Kristi, plus another friend from church, Marcia, were both going to counseling sessions at the same Christian counseling center. Because I could see both of these older sisters speaking true revelations and going through their own healing metamorphosis, I figured that the center must be a good place.

My first appointment at the Oak Brook Christian Counseling Center was in a small, windowless but homey room in the basement of a storefront located in a small nearby suburb, Westmont. Annie Lafrentz walked into the little room and brightened everything with her warm smile and loving presence. What I didn't know yet was that in that place I would gain not only an amazing therapist and friend, but also the emotional mother I had lost years earlier. On that day, Annie began to finish raising me where Mom had left off when she got sick. I had a mom again, and what a mom!

The first thing we worked on, which took quite a while, was my relationship with Mom. Annie specialized in codependency, and she lovingly and logically helped me to understand the difference between caring for Mom and caring about Mom, as I had been trying to take over God's job as Mom's healer. God did not desire that I give up marrying, having children, and tending to my own needs to grieve in order to "help" my mother.

And so I broke up with Mom. At least it felt similar to a breakup. By this time, Mom had become extremely dependent on me. It felt like 100 percent of my energy was given to serving her, and none of her energy came back to me. It was very unbalanced. Mom had become childish and completely self-focused. I always felt emotionally drained after visiting her, and I usually numbed and rewarded myself with food afterward.

So I told Mom that I needed to have a more give-and-take relationship with her, rather than just me giving and her taking. Needless to say, my selfish, self-absorbed mother didn't like that at all. I cut back on the number of visits and cut back on the hours, too, and I let myself have a social life of my own. Then. one day as we spoke on the phone, Mom told me she was going to kill herself. I knew, though, that this was merely an attempt to draw me back in to being her caretaker. She hadn't threatened suicide since her in-and-out-of-Elgin days, nearly ten years earlier. This was just another manipulative effort. So, I told her, "Well, Mom, I would be disappointed if you did try to kill yourself, but that's your decision. That's your choice." The other end of the line was silent: Mom was surprised that her attempt had failed so badly. And that was the last time my mother ever threatened suicide.

But she continued to try to get me to spend all of my attention on her, without reciprocity. As if I were teaching a toddler that the world did not revolve around her, I had to teach this to my fifty-five-year-old mother by never rewarding selfishness. Without Annie's love, insight, and encouragement, I would never have had the strength to say no to my demanding, adult-sized child mom.

From my journals:

October 1, 1989

Detachment is the pits. I hope this is good. It's so hard. I just told my mom I wouldn't see her on a Saturday but on a Tuesday night. Even though it was her idea and she understands, it really hurts. I hate disappointing her. But I am sick of giving up all my Saturdays for her. I just want to be free from this bondage, this yoke. I want to live my own life. I don't want to be tied down to her. Saturdays are the only day I have to do errands, clean, call people, work on projects around the house, take a bike ride, pay bills, etc. I have spent every other Saturday with her FOR TEN YEARS of my youth!!!!! They're gone. I gave my lifeblood.

I know that, as I pull away, it can eventually help her to better her own life. I hope she will.

She is really trying. That hurts the most. That she loves me so much to understand, to cooperate, to even sacrifice herself for me. It's so hard for me to take. I hate backing off. I feel so bad for her. I don't want her to be lonely. And I just love her so much. I just feel so bad. I am tempted to give in and not follow through on this hard detachment process. But I really am sick of the bondage and I don't want to live like this the rest of my life. I don't think I should have to pay for her life with mine—especially because I can't really make it all better anyway.

December 21, 1989

I had my second meeting with Annie tonight. When I talked to Annie about my feelings in letting go, I realized I am letting go of the only sense of security that I have.

I know how to be Mom's care person. But I am not too familiar with being me. So, I am more secure with my role. I am now risking losing that. Plus, I am neurotically afraid of what will happen to her. Her track record isn't too good. How do I get healed of my fear? I guess like all other fears—face them. Maybe they'll happen. Probably they won't. My heart needs to feel and face what will be.

January 23, 1990

Codependency is sticky business—I have sticky glue hanging on me as I pull away.

I ended up not even seeing Mom through Thanksgiving, Christmas, Easter, and even the following Mother's Day. For the first time, Mom spent the holidays without me. It was traumatic for both of us. I wanted to see her, but Mom kept trying to control me and get me to sacrifice myself for her. She would not agree to anything I asked for and just wanted everything her way. I remember for my birthday she actually wanted me to buy *her* presents and take her out! So I stood my ground and waited for her to realize I had really changed, and if she wanted a relationship with me, she better change, too. My stubborn mother fought for months and months, but she finally shifted and started tending to me, no longer just taking from me. Turned out, it was the right move. Mom and I grew and healed.

Before the breakup, Mom would never venture away from the nursing home without me by her side. Afterward, Mom somehow learned to go out by herself, walking or taking a bus, taxi, or "Dial a Ride" to wherever she wanted to go. She became free.

December 16, 1989

Mom called "Dial a Ride"! She has been going out shopping on her own!

January 23, 1990

Mom asked me to bring piano music—she wants to start playing again. She's growing, too! Yeah!

Before the breakup, I was Mom's only friend. Afterward, she reached out to residents and staff at the nursing home, and even had a couple of boyfriends her age. Old friends from the past reconnected with her, as did her sisters. I got out of the way, and freed Mom to have a community of people who cared about her.

Before the changes I made, I had paid for everything Mom wanted. Afterward, she took jobs at the home delivering mail and newspapers, working in their "country store," earning a little bit of her own money and a large quantity of self-satisfaction. She proudly started to buy her own clothes and meals.

It turned out that in all my efforts to help Mom, I had been hurting her. Mom was much more capable, even with schizophrenia, than I had given her credit for. And not only did Mom heal, I did too.

After I started counseling, I created a list of changes I had made as a result, and I kept adding to it over the years of therapy. Below is a sampling from the list of 175 changes that shows the evolutionary process I went through during this time in my life because of letting go of Mom and letting myself heal.

1. *Stopped spending every other Saturday afternoon and evening taking my mother to Jewel, K-Mart, Ponderosa, and anywhere else she wanted to go, and paying for her dinner!*

2. *Planted tomato plants.*

3. *Rearranged my furniture.*

4. *Redecorated my apartment.*

5. *Bought a beautiful new, expensive car!*

6. *Spent a lot of money!*

7. *Developed a budget and live by it now.*

8. *Planned financial goals and am working towards them.*

9. *Bought clothes—spent a lot of $.*

10. *Bought clothes that don't try to hide my shape but instead, accent me—with color! Style! Stopped*

wearing jeans in summer—now wear short skirts. Traded tennis shoes in for sandals.

11. *Experimented with hair styles until I found one that really looks good.*

12. *Went to a male hairdresser just to be around a man, which turned into a very positive relationship.*

13. *Learned to identify my feelings and get them out. Learned to cry, be fearful, be angry, etc. And learned to deal with pain.*

14. *Gave up fatty foods—lost weight.*

15. *Ended an eight-year best friendship with a verbally abusive, everything is wrong with me according to her, friend.*

16. *Became a more focused, hard worker.*

17. *Joined a singles group.*

18. *Took an acting class.*

19. *Made new friends.*

20. *Learned to deal with angry people—and not take on their anger. Learned to feel good about myself no matter how angry others get.*

21. *Learned to speak up and defend myself!*

22. *Stopped worrying about what my grandparents think or demand and just gave up trying to please them.*

23. *Learned who I can talk to about what.*

24. *Stopped waiting for my birthday and Christmas to get things I want. Learned to spend money on me, when I want.*

25. *Continued to learn "Who is Sandy?" and to like her.*

26. *Learned how to play.*

27. *Learned how to relax.*

28. *Started actually believing the good things that people say about me.*

29. *Learned to identify what I want and need, to voice it, and to give it to myself.*

30. *Learned to enjoy my sense of humor, and laugh more.*

31. *Learned to have boundaries in relationships.*

32. *Didn't spend all my vacation days traveling.*

33. *Began oil painting.*

34. *Learned that I was afraid of men, and so started being more vulnerable to men.*

35. *Bought a CD player—something I had wanted for years but wouldn't buy for myself.*

36. *Realized that I am attractive, even when I'm overweight.*

37. *Started asking my church to pray for me. Learned to receive and be vulnerable. Learned to trust people who knew of my struggles.*

38. *Learned not to be so hard on myself.*

39. *Decided to face my fear of men, and try to meet men who will be right for me, trust them and date.*

40. *Learned to pray daily for myself.*

41. *Learned to really listen to the compliments people gave me and let them help me love myself better.*

42. *Learned that I am special.*

43. *Learned to stop taking leadership roles in everything because I felt I had to be a leader if I wanted to be liked. (I couldn't just be Sandy. That wasn't good enough.)*

44. *Learned to receive from others and give to myself.*

45. *Went on a date.*

46. *Lost 28 pounds, and continue to drop extra weight.*

47. *Decided to buy a home—and did!*

48. *Like myself a lot more.*

49. *Stopped playing softball with women. Started playing it with men!*

50. *Realized that people do like me.*

51. *Asked a guy out.*

52. *Lost 35 pounds.*

53. *Didn't spend Thanksgiving, Christmas, any birthdays, Mother's Day or any other holidays with my mom.*

54. *Realized my dream and went to Greece.*

55. *Read a lot of self-help books:*
    a. *The Road Less Traveled*
    b. *Fat Is a Feminist Issue*
    c. *One-Way Relationships*
    d. *Women's Reality*
    e. *Healing the Child Within*
    f. *Healing the Shame that Binds You*
    g. *People of the Lie*
    h. *Always Daddy's Girl*
    i. *Schizophrenia Book*
    j. *Wounded Woman*
    k. *The Pleasers*
    l. *Healing the Dysfunctional Church Family*
    m. *Women Who Love Too Much*
    n. *It Will Never Happen to Me*
    o. *Women at the Well*

56. *Began reading romance novels to help me desire romance.*

57. *Developed more assertiveness in making female friends.*

58. *Stopped being a complainer at work at started taking initiative.*

59. Experienced my mom treating me to dinner, including appetizers, at Red Lobster, and then she took me to a store and let me pick out my own blouse and bought it for my birthday.

60. Fell in love.

61. Dated lots of men.

62. Bought a sequined dress.

63. Hired an interior decorator.

64. Bought a mandolin.

65. Took decorating classes and decorated my home.

66. Took a synthesizer class and guitar lessons.

67. Played piano for the dinner music at a public dinner.

68. Was hired to be the pianist for a conference in Chattanooga.

69. Was proposed to.

70. Have two-way friendships, and not one-way.

71. Cried in front of a man.

72. Took up golf.

73. Dated 10 guys in one year! Really worked on dating and got over my fears.

74. Learned how to flirt and be assertive with men.

75. Learned to keep my work life in perspective, and not be so rigid about rules.

76. Learned to have a balanced attitude in dating— not expecting guys to be not good enough or too good, but accepting them as humans; accepting me and staying loyal to me in the dating process; learned to not shame myself if a relationship doesn't happen.

Chapter 14

PEACE

November 11, 1996

> *I like Don. He's cute. It's hard to believe he's 40. I really like him. I wonder what will happen . . . He told me he wishes he married me instead of his ex-wife. He thought that after our first date.*
>
> *He's such a little guy. Is he too little? At least he's got some meat on his bones. But I'm hardly perfect. He doesn't seem to mind that I'm so heavy.*
>
> *He's so soft-spoken. I find that to be challenging— he's hard to hear, but inviting too. I feel I can trust him.*
>
> *I'm not sure if he is assertive enough or confident enough. I think he is, just in a quiet way. I think he is going to be very good for me.*
>
> *Maybe I'll actually marry this guy. Wouldn't that be amazing? Already I'm developing feelings for him. I suppose it's mostly infatuation. But it feels good just the same.*
>
> *I finally believe love is for me. I, too, can be loved by a man. I, too, am entitled to love. Yay and Yippee!*

AFTER FREEING MYSELF from Mom, and her from me, I was finally able to tend to myself. And I discovered that I had stopped growing, as a person, when I became her caretaker, beginning at age fourteen.

And so in my thirties, I now got to live the way I should have during my teen and young adult years. I started to figure out how I wanted to dress, breaking out of a closet of beige into a world of color and expression in fashion. I experimented with different looks, like a teenager leaning to apply makeup for the first time. I had a very interesting big-earring stage (I'm still burning the photos!). I started dating, and risking myself emotionally with men. I picked up my guitar and started singing, not just in the safety of my home and little church, but in public places, like restaurants and coffeehouses. I bought my own home and started having my own life.

At age thirty-six, I joined a cheap dating service, and for the fifty-dollar fee, I was set up with a divorced man with shoulder-length brown hair who had the most caring eyes I had ever seen in a man. Less than two years later I found myself at the altar, singing him a love song I wrote: we had just taken our marriage vows to each other. And along with him, I received the honor of loving his three kids and, later, our two precious granddaughters. Certainly that was the best fifty bucks I ever spent!

Don and me on our wedding day, August 16, 1998.

After we first met, Don had told me that his two younger teenage children were living with his ex-wife, who had unmedicated bipolar disorder and was an alcoholic. We learned later she was also using drugs. I told Don how deeply disturbing it was for me to be a teenager and live with a mom with an untreated mental illness. I told him he had to get them out of that situation, and that it was probably much worse than he feared. Don believed me, but he didn't have any grounds to get custody of the children.

So we joined together in prayer. Our first answer came one day when his ex called him out of the blue and said, "I can't

Mom holding our oldest granddaughter, Alexis, when she was less than one month old.

take Kristyn anymore. You take her!" And—poof—Don's daughter, Kristyn, came to live with Don, just like that. We think Don's ex was attempting to scare me away from marrying him, because the incident occurred while we were engaged. But having Kristyn live with her father was exactly what Don and I earnestly wanted. It wasn't legal custody yet, and his youngest child, Danny, was still living with his mother.

So, on the following Monday we decided to both fast and pray for two meals, during breakfast and lunch, asking God to somehow work it out so Don could gain permanent custody of both Kristyn and Danny. At the end of our fast on that very day, Don got a call during which he learned that his ex-wife, who practiced witchcraft, had tried to cast a spell which involved igniting a stack of Bibles and burning a pentagon into the floor. She then slit her wrists. She had started the indoor fire while Danny was sleeping in the next room, and the fire, at least, threatened his life. She was checked into the psychiatric ward of the local hospital, and Danny went to live with Don that same day.

The temporary custody hearing two weeks later lasted five minutes. Don's lawyer said that it was the fastest custody hearing he'd ever had. The permanent custody hearing a month later lasted less than a half hour. Don had all the evidence he needed to gain full custody, and his ex-wife had no sensible rebuttal.

After Don and I married, the adjustment was difficult for all of us. Some women wouldn't have taken on teenage step-kids, but I had prayed for it and was happy to be their step-mom, even if they weren't so sure about me. I knew firsthand what they had lived through, and I knew Don and I had to do all in our power to help them. And so we did. Because of what I had gone through with Mom, I was open to welcoming teens into my life, loving them, and making them my own family. I got more family from the loss of my own.

And now Mom has more family, too. She loves her new son-in-law, and she adores my mother-in-law. She now has more people in her life to love, and to love her, because I let myself have love.

Since Mom adjusted to our give-and-take relationship, she has been part of every holiday and family event year after year, enriching our family with her sweet and quirky love.

Mom has been on medication ever since her first institutionalization at Elgin in 1979, but for many years, the medication only reduced her paranoia. In the 1990s, new drugs became available that have turned out to be quite effective for Mom, and since then I have rarely heard Mom utter a paranoid word. Most people who meet her now can't tell that she has schizophrenia. She and I talk or see each other at least weekly, much like any mother and daughter would, and our conversations are two-way. I truly enjoy her company.

Although Mom didn't get to live her adult life in her own apartment with a job and normal hobbies and interests, she did have a home for over thirty years where people looked out for her. Countryside Healthcare Center's caring staff made sure she had everything she needed—food, medical attention, a comfortable bed, and social interactions. Then I was free to have my own life and be there for her emotionally, but without the responsibility for her every need. As a result, at nearly eighty years old, Mom has lived far longer than most people with this debilitating disease, and she has had a life full of love and connecting even with it.

A person with treated schizophrenia can be pretty wonderful. Mom has impressed me so many times when I have told her about the events of my life, and she has responded with incredibly insightful words, motherly encouragement, understanding, and affirmation. She comes through more and more. In the most surprising ways and at the most surprising times, Mom is often the wisest person I know. It has made me wonder what mental illness and sanity really are. Disease, even a mental one, does not necessarily imply mental unhealth, any more than a freedom from disease equals a healthy mental state. It's what you do with what you get. It's who you are. It's about love. Love creates the ultimate mental health. And today, Mom and I are full of both.

Me, Mom and Don, Christmas 2003.

Mom with her grandchildren, Dan and Allison (Ted's kids).

Mom with Ted's wife, Mary, and Allison

Mom at my nephew Dan's First Communion party.

Mom and Me at Ted's wedding in 1993. She sewed her lace dress entirely by hand. I bought mine at a store.

One of many sweet Mother's days with Mom.
I'm grateful for every one.

Mom and me on the day we spread Grandma Hartman's ashes at Morton Arboretum. I am 33 and Mom is 57.

Me and Don.

Chapter 15

ENJOYING THE VIEW

WHEN I FIRST dealt with Mom's strange way of looking at the world, my reactions usually were of shock, embarrassment, and confusion because I was often disturbed and upset by it. But over the years, I gradually learned to accept that Mom simply has a different view of the world. Instead of fighting it, I thought, why not enjoy the view? So now I do. And Mom gives me a steady flow of pleasure as a result. Before my marriage, I introduced Mom to one of my boyfriends, and I told her that he didn't understand why I wanted so many shoes.

"Can you explain to him why we like shoes, Mom?" Mom articulated our rationale so well: "Well, when your feet look good, you feel good." I was delighted and said, "Yes, yes! That's exactly it!" Then Mom said, "Well, looks like I'm your shoe lawyer."

Mom has a lovely, off-center, delightful way of seeing the world and expressing herself. When she met Don, my eventual husband, she said, "Well, he is so cute. Yes, you should date him. He's a wonderful thing to do."

Mom's advice can range from completely "on" and fantastic—better than that of the supposedly sane people in my life—to wondrously bizarre. For example, Don had colon cancer for a number of years. One time, after he took Mom home after a holiday, he came into the house and reported to me, "Your mom told me that to get over cancer, all I need to do is drink a glass of milk." Mom always was a milk pusher, but this was a whole new level of application. We had a great laugh at Mom's off-kilter way of loving.

Mom has had lots of "boyfriends" at the nursing home, even into her late seventies. There was the ninety-nine-year-old man she "dated" until he died. And then there was Chester. She really liked talking to Chester after supper every evening. Then one day, I visited her and said, "How's the boyfriend Mom?" "Oh, he's history," the heartbreaker replied. "Why is that, Mom?" I pushed. "Oh, he just doesn't do it for me anymore," she said. What a far cry from the need to almost literally "jump" out of a relationship as she had in her past. Mom found her voice, speaking her likes and dislikes, versus the old life of being used and abused.

I call Mom every week to check in. One week the conversation gave me my usual chuckle.

"Helloooo?" Mom answered.

"Hi Mom, it's me. How are you?"

"Well, not too good. This cranky old man keeps crashing into me with his walker."

"Oh, sorry to hear that Mom."

"Yeah, his wife brought him in because he was acting goofy."

Dad was never a religious man, but as he aged, and after he was diagnosed with cancer and heart disease, he started every day with a simple prayer: "Thank you, Lord, for another day." I told Mom that Dad had this new spiritual habit and she responded, "Yeah, he's cramming for the test!"

Every time Mom calls me, she starts the conversation with, "Hello, this is your mother, Susie G in Aurora." I know her voice, and yet she feels she has to give her name and city for me to know who she is! So funny. She signs her cards the same way.

Mom once sweetly sent a get-well card for my husband. But because she wasn't able to buy a get-well card from the store, she improvised with a card she had already purchased. Funny how she decided to modify it—by writing between the printed lines instead of on all the space on the inside of the card. She wrote: *"I will go look at mail, probably on Holiday or Tuesday. I enjoyed my Bag of beef, bread and fries for supper here with a milk and 2 small apricots in a cup. This is a Get Well as you are like son, and good wishes. Thank you & Sandy for the neat Birthday. I was 72. It looks like a plain week here—We train a new receptionist (hopefully). Love Mom Susie (Georg)."* We loved the card. Mom's innocent expressions are priceless, like those of a child who means no harm, but really doesn't know how adults do things.

November 12, 2008

Dear Dan,

I will go look at mail, probably on Holiday or Tuesday. I enjoyed my Bag of beef, bread + few fries for supper

Sending cheerful thoughts

here with a milk and 2 small apri-

and caring wishes

cats in a cup.

to help make your day

This is a Get Well as you are

a little bit brighter.

able Dan, and good wishes

Thank you + Sandy for the neat Birthday. I was 72. It looks like a plain week here — we train a new Receptionist (hopefully.)

Love Mom Susie
(Georg)

Check out her rating of me as a daughter in the following card.

September 14
2008

Dear Sandy,
       To the Best Daughter in Illinois.
Just my way of keeping in touch.
    My prayers are with you for
Wednesday and Best Wishes for
September, and good health.
                    Love, Susie Gr
                        Mother

Not the best daughter in the world, just in Illinois.

Another time, when she was in the hospital and not permitted to eat or drink due to a procedure she was about to receive, she got very upset and said, "When I get out of here, I'm going to get on the board of directors and be sure there is food and drink for everyone in this hospital!" The nurse and I had a warm giggle at her confident rebellion. On another day, when my brother was with her and she couldn't eat or drink before a medical test, she said to Ted, "Cover your ears," then yelled loudly at the nurses, "Bring me a drink! It's OK, you'll still get paid!" My brother fought back laughter. Good thing he was warned to cover his ears!

Could it be possible Mom was slightly over protective? I mean, where is my face?

Then there was the time Mom was recovering from surgery and had me bring her lunch—a McDonald's cheeseburger and plain ice cream sundae. She loved the food but then found herself with an upset stomach, and threw up the meal. As I was cleaning her, she happily said of the vomit: "That tastes good." I guess I should be happy my company's product tastes good both going down and coming back up again. Not sure if we'll make that a marketing slogan, though!

Then there was the time Mom said, after a holiday meal, "Oh Sandy, that was such a great meal. That was the best dinner I ever had." I really felt good until the next meal and many others following it: after every one, Mom declared, "That was the best meal I ever had!" Don and I began to laughingly express that same compliment when we cooked for each other, even after a simple meal like Hamburger Helper.

On a visit with Mom she asked me for a dollar, saying "I just want to look at it." Never thought a dollar bill could be so entertaining.

One of many of Mom's birthday celebrations.

Ted gave Mom candy for her birthday one year, to which she replied, "Oh good! Candy! They've been serving us nothing but water and toast for a week."

For one Mother's Day occasion, we had not only my husband's kids and granddaughters over, but my stepdaughter's in-laws, who didn't know Mom well. Don and I gave Mom a nice white summer shirt with ruffles. She wasn't sure if it would fit and said she needed to try it on. Instead of waiting until later or going into another room, Mom just started pulling off clothes right in front of everyone. A knot formed in my stomach as I anticipated that I would have to intervene if Mom took off too many layers. My stepdaughter's teenage sister-in-law was completely appalled to see Mom undress. Everyone else, though, had a huge grin, knowing that this was just my sweet but odd mom. Fortunately, she stopped undressing with a couple of layers to go, put on the shirt, and declared it a winner. I let out a sigh of relief, and we all found ourselves forcing back laughter. It's a great memory for all of us. We call it the Mother's Day Striptease.

I visit Mom weekly, bringing her dinner from McDonald's—her favorite. We look at clothes in catalogs, then play three hands of rummy, and I try very hard to let Mom win. One week it seemed she was forcing me to win. "What'd you get?" I asked after each hand. "Thirty-five," was her reply every time. How do you get exactly thirty-five points every time in rummy? And that week she was actually a good loser, which isn't like Mom. Then as I left and told her good-bye, she said, "Love you. And fix your hair!" What a way to send me off.

Mom was a fun mom. Here she is sledding with us.

A few years back, Don and I came to take Mom out on a Sunday for her birthday. She said she had heard about a great restaurant, and she had the directions, so she guided us there. It was a divey bar-and-grill in a residential neighborhood. I said, "These places sometimes have good food. Let's give it a try!" Mom said, "I heard it was really good." In we went. After a little while a big, long-bearded biker dressed head to toe in black leather and tattoos came in and sat at the bar. Then another, then another, until tough-looking bikers filled the bar. Turns out we were eating at a biker bar, and that was their meeting place before their big Sunday ride. I looked outside, and in the parking lot I counted over 60 bikes. Absolutely comical. Mom told one of the bikers that it was her birthday. He yelled, "Hey everybody, this is Susan, and it's her birthday. Let's sing to her." The whole place erupted in a round of "Happy Birthday to You." Don and I looked at each other with an "Is this really happening?" kind of look and grinned with delight. Life is an adventure with Mom. A great adventure.

Mom also seems to lack the filters the rest of us apply to our daily speech. I can't tell you how many

Mom playing with us in the snow. I'm the one who can't keep up.

times we have been out to dinner and Mom has started telling the server her entire life story, about being an alcoholic, about having certain embarrassing diseases, about her love life. No topic is taboo for Mom. At first it embarrassed me, but now I find it fun to watch the server's reaction. Most are incredibly gracious and smile warmly at her funny openness.

Then there was another memorable time when Don picked her up from her nursing home to bring her to our home while I cooked a big holiday meal. Mom told Don she needed to make a stop in the bathroom, and then disappeared for what seemed an eternity. Finally emerging, Mom said in her inappropriate manner, "Sorry it took me so long. It was a big one!"

I love her view.

Mom continues to bring smiles and laughter, and she also has brought me a lifetime of love. A conversation rarely ends without a mutual "I love you," just like in any other loving mother-daughter relationship. When we are in a store, she will point me to a clothes item and say, "What do you think of this? Let's get it for you." She always wants to give me beautiful clothes, which to her is one of the greatest acts of love possible. When I am in tears over a loss, I can count on her to say, "It'll work out Sandy. It'll be all right." And you know, she is right: it does.

Our journey together has been challenging for us both, but I know that one of God's greatest acts of love toward me was when he gave me Mom. I am a better person because of her.

My beautiful mom, age 79

Chapter 16

MAKING A DIFFERENCE

*"The prevalence of homelessness in persons with severe
mental illness, including schizophrenia, is
distressingly high."* [27]

*"Managed care for people with schizophrenia has not
expanded as much as for the remainder of the
U.S. health sector"* [28]

MY FRIENDS AND I were sightseeing in Washington, D.C.,
when we encountered a large, hairy, apparently homeless man
sitting on a park bench. He seemed to be out of his mind on a
drug trip. We went to eat, and I purchased an extra sandwich to
give to the man in case he was still there when we were finished
with our meal. He was, and when I handed the sandwich to
him, he grabbed it quickly and said nothing as he worked on
figuring out how to open the packaging so he could eat the food.
Although I was glad to help him, I felt sad that he seemed to be
just barely living.

27　Alan Felix, Dan Herman, and Ezra Susser, "Housing Instability and Homelessness,"
in *Clinical Handbook of Schizophrenia*, ed. Kim T. Mueser and Dilip V. Jeste (New York:
Guilford, 2008), 412.

28　Mihail Samnaliev and Robin E. Clark, "The Economics of Schizophrenia," in
Clinical Handbook of Schizophrenia, ed. Kim T. Mueser and Dilip V. Jeste (New York:
Guilford, 2008), 514.

Unfortunately, a large percentage of people with schizophrenia live at least part of their lives without a home. This trend increased significantly after the 1960s, when public policy began calling for persons with mental illnesses to be integrated into society, rather than living in institutions. Efforts to aid persons in this transition were lacking, and over time, assistance has fallen far behind the need. Consequently, persons with significant mental illnesses do not have enough resources available to help them cope with their challenges. Today, due to governmental budget cuts and reduced charitable giving, the situation is worsening.

One of the most significant challenges faced by people with disabilities who are unable to keep a regular job is how costly housing is. The National Alliance on Mental Illness (NAMI) reported in 2011 that the average monthly SSI payment of $703 per month is less than the average rent for a modest one-bedroom apartment in most of the United States.[29] One might think that the disabled person could solve this problem by working occasionally or by receiving help from friends, family, or a faith community. But in most cases, if an SSI beneficiary earns income to help meet the cost of housing or receives financial support from others, the SSI payment decreases. It is very difficult for many people with disabilities to maintain an income high enough to meet the cost of housing—not to mention other necessities like clothing, toiletries, and medical costs.

Of course, the gap between income and housing costs means that many people with severe disabilities have a difficult time securing stable housing, so it is not unusual for people with mental illness to become homeless, and living on the streets with schizophrenia has a number of appalling consequences. In addition to suffering from inadequate nutrition and exposure

29   National Alliance on Mental Illness, "New Priced Out Report Released: Critical Advocacy Tool for Expanding Access to Affordable Housing for People Living with Mental Illness," June 20, 2011, https://www2.nami.org/Template.cfm?Section=Issue_Spotlights&template=/ContentManagement/ContentDisplay.cfm&ContentID=122715. SSI is Supplemental Security Income for people with disabilities who cannot work consistently. "Supplemental" is a misnomer: a person who has assets of over $2,000 is not eligible for SSI, and employment income exceeding $85 per month triggers a reduction in the SSI payment. Loved ones of a person with a disability can set up an OBRA Special Needs Trust to help with expenses in a way that won't trigger a reduction in benefits, but setting up a trust can be expensive, and loved ones often are unaware of this option or do not have resources to contribute such a fund.

to the elements, homeless people are at risk of violence. Up to one-third of homeless women with schizophrenia have been raped, and 66 percent of these have been raped multiple times;[30] some women report having been raped as many as 17 times.[31] Of course such violence can and does worsen their illness, and reduce the likelihood that their condition will improve. Rape also causes a higher risk of HIV because many of the men who rape schizophrenic, homeless women are drug addicts, among whom HIV infection is common.[32] Worse yet, people who are "homeless and suffering from a psychiatric illness have a markedly elevated death rate from a variety of causes."[33]

People who are homeless are often arrested for trespassing or other offenses and sentenced to jail or prison. This happens so frequently to people with severe psychiatric disabilities that

> Prisons and jails have become America's "new asylums": The number of individuals with serious mental illness in prisons and jails now exceeds the number in state psychiatric hospitals tenfold. Most of the mentally ill individuals in prisons and jails would have been treated in state psychiatric hospitals in the years before the deinstitutionalization movement led to closing the hospitals, a trend that continues even today.[34]

Essentially, prison administrators throughout the United States have found themselves running mental institutions, but without the tools and resources to provide the care that people

---

30   W. R. Breakey, P. J. Fischer, M. Kramer, G. Nestadt, A. J. Romanoski, A. Ross, R. M. Royall, and O.C. Stine. "Health and Mental Health Problems of Homeless Men and Women in Baltimore," *Journal of the American Medical Association* 262:1352–57

31   C. J. Cooper, "Brutal Lives of Homeless S.F. Women," *San Francisco Examiner,* December 18, 1988.

32   Treatment Advocacy Center, "Homelessness: Tragic Side Effect of Non-Treatment," n.d., http://newyorkcity.ny.networkofcare.org/mh/library/article.aspx?id=369.

33   R. E. Drake, M. A. Wallach, and J. S. Hoffman, "Housing Instability and Homelessness among Aftercare Patients in an Urban State Hospital," *Hospital and Community Psychiatry* 40 (1989): 46–51.

34   Treatment Advocacy Center, *The Treatment of Persons with Mental Illness in Prisons and Jails: A State Survey, Treatment,* April 18, 2004, p. 6, http://tacreports.org/storage/documents/treatment-behind-bars/treatment-behind-bars.pdf.

with mental illness need. Prisons simply are not designed to help people with psychiatric disabilities. Furthermore, individuals with mental illness are particularly vulnerable to being beaten or raped while incarcerated. Because prisoners' psychiatric illnesses aren't adequately treated, their condition often worsens, and they leave prison sicker than when they entered.

Some people do recover from schizophrenia. Over 50 percent either improve substantially or recover completely, and about 25 percent live relatively independent lives.[35] But these are the people who are treated and helped, not those who are left to their own devices financially and medically, and who become vulnerable to repeated bouts of violence, homelessness, hospitalization, and incarceration. A combination of community mental health services, access to medical care, income support, and truly affordable housing can augment mentally ill persons' own hard work toward recovery and the supportive efforts of their families and friends.

These services and supports cost money, but not nearly as much money as the alternatives. Mark Ishuag, CEO of Thresholds, Illinois' largest provider of recovery services to people with mental illness, quickly gets to the bottom line in a statement opposing Illinois governor Bruce Rauner's proposed cuts to mental health services: "The annual per person cost to house someone with a serious mental illness at Cook County Jail is $69,350. In contrast, a full year of the most intensive level of community-based treatment costs just $10,243, and a rental housing voucher for a year costs just $9,200."[36] People in crisis who visit some Chicago emergency rooms will see the cost of psychiatric hospitalization posted prominently on the wall of the waiting room: over $2,000 per night. Obviously, community-based treatment and housing, which can prevent incarceration and reduce the number of hospitalizations, is a much more financially responsible solution than cutting community mental health services. Nevertheless, these services are on the

---

35   E. Fuller Torrey, *Surviving Schizophrenia: A Manual for Families, Patients, and Providers*, (New York: Harper-Collins Publishers, 2006), 106.

36   "Thresholds CEO Mark Ishaug Speaks Out against Costly Mental Health Budget Cuts," May 20, 2015, http://www.thresholds.org/2015/05/thresholds-ceo-mark-ishaug-speaks-out-against-costly-mental-health-budget-cuts/.

chopping block in states and localities throughout the United States—regardless of which political party is in power. In 2012, for example, half of Chicago's public mental health clinics were closed down under the leadership Mayor Rahm Emmanuel.

Some people with schizophrenia are fortunate enough to have parents who provide housing and care for them. But in some families, like mine, the illness is too much for the parents to handle, or schizophrenic adults outlive their caretaker parents. Some folks with schizophrenia live on their own, but many cannot. Group homes can be ideal for some people with mental illnesses, but there are not enough of them.

Mom was blessed to have a good nursing home take her in. But it was working with Mom. Most of the people living there were significantly older than she was, and the old folks she got to know would eventually die. A nursing home is not the best environment for a person with a mental illness.

Then there was the awful day when Mom was in the hospital for a short stay, and I was told she would need to stay longer, because she needed surgery. I called Countryside to let them know about the extension. To my shock, the assistant administrator told me the home could not guarantee that a bed would be available for her after her hospitalization, even though Mom's things were still in her room and no one had moved into it. Countryside had been Mom's home for over twenty-seven years. She had only been in the hospital for nine days at that point, and they were threatening to kick her out! I was livid. Most likely the reason for this callous response was that Mom was on public aid, and the State of Illinois was not timely in paying its bills. If the home could replace Mom with a private-pay patient, they could both charge more and receive the funds more rapidly.

After researching other homes and talking with the wonderful people at NAMI, I followed up the next day with the head administrator at Countryside. I gave her an earful regarding the injustice of their choice, and she backed down. Countryside continued to provide a bed for Mom, and now she was in her first private room.

What if Mom hadn't had me to fight for her? Something is very wrong with our society if a person can live a secure and happy life in a home for twenty-seven years, providing a constant income via payments from the government, and that home has the ability to kick her out any time if she gets too sick. We need to fix this. We need to provide safe places for people with these debilitating illnesses to live happy lives.

How can you help? Simply put: donate. We can empower great organizations like NAMI to pour private funds into research, and we can encourage our leaders to contribute government funds to research, housing, and services to help these folks. Below is a list of organizations that are working at providing housing and better answers for people with schizophrenia.

And I can't end this book without encouraging you to do one more thing: love. I hope that, as you've walked through my journey with Mom, you have learned to love her as I do, and therefore to love people who have schizophrenia. They need our love. And we need theirs.

"And now these three remain: faith, hope and love.
But the greatest of these is love."

1 Corinthians 13:13

Housing Organizations

Supportive Housing Providers Association
4 West Old State Capitol Plaza, Suite 820
Springfield, IL 62701
217-528-9814 (Springfield)
312-202-0254 (Chicago)
www.shpa-il.org

Thresholds
4101 N. Ravenswood Ave.
Chicago, IL 60613
773-572-5400
www.thresholds.org

Advocacy Organizations
National Alliance on Mental Illness (NAMI)
3803 N. Fairfax Dr., Ste. 100
Arlington, VA 22203
800-950-NAMI (6264)
www.nami.org

Research Organizations
Alexian Brothers Center for Mental Health
3436 N. Kennicott Ave.
Arlington Heights, IL 60004
847-952-7460
www.alexianbrothershealth.org

Rush University Medical Center
Depression Treatment and Research Center
1700 W. Van Buren St., 5th floor
Chicago, IL 60612
312-942-6597
www.rush.edu/services/depression-treatment-and-
research-center

University of Illinois at Chicago
Department of Psychiatry
Neuropsychiatric Institute
912 S. Wood Street (M/C 913)
Chicago, IL 60612
Principal investigator: Peter Weiden
312-996-9986
pweiden@psych.uic.edu

Midwest Center for Neurobehavioral Medicine
18W100 22nd Street
Oakbrook Terrace, IL 60181
(630) 705-1501

Northwestern University Feinberg School of Medicine
Department of Psychiatry and Behavioral Sciences
Onterie Center
446 East Ontario, Suite 7-200
Chicago, Illinois 60611
312-926-2323
http://psychiatry.northwestern.edu

GSK Clinical Trials
877-379-3718
GSKClinicalSupportHD@gsk.com

Chapter 17

POSTLUDE

IN 2004, MY HUSBAND Don was diagnosed with colorectal cancer. When I told Mom, she lovingly encouraged me saying, "It'll be all right, Sandy. God will help you through it." She was in our corner. Don had radiation, major surgery, and four months of chemo. But the cancer returned, and in 2006 he was given three years to live. I entered a grieving period unlike any other I had experienced before. At first, Mom struggled to believe such a grim prognosis, but in time she accepted the situation as I did, and encouraged me saying, "It'll be all right, Sandy. Try not to worry too much." Don did live much longer than expected, but in 2012 he passed away from the cancer. Mom just said, "I'm so sorry." She came to the wake, supporting me once again when I needed her. As I went through my time of mourning, Mom called me often to see how I was and to encourage me, saying "It'll be all right Sandy. Come over, bring some McDonald's and let's play some cards." Then, on March 31, 2014, I met a new special man, Roger, who I married the following year. Mom was elated. And just as she had welcomed and loved my first sweet husband, Don, she welcomed my second gem of a man, Roger. Many wish they had just one special love in their life. I feel deeply blessed to have gotten to love and be loved by two great men. And many people desire a loving and close relationship with their mom. Amazingly, even with living with schizophrenia, Mom and I have had a close, healthy and loving lifelong relationship. I know I am truly blessed.

"He is able to do exceedingly abundantly above all that we ask or imagine."

Ephesians 3:20

Me and my second love, Roger.
Forever Thankful.

CPSIA information can be obtained
at www.ICGtesting.com
Printed in the USA
FSOW04n2140241016
26541FS

9 781633 932791